JAMES LAWRENCE ISHERWOOD

(1917-1989)

A biography by Dr Brian Iddon

JAMES LAWRENCE ISHERWOOD

(1917-1989)

A biography by Dr Brian Iddon

MEMOIRS

Cirencester

Published by Memoirs

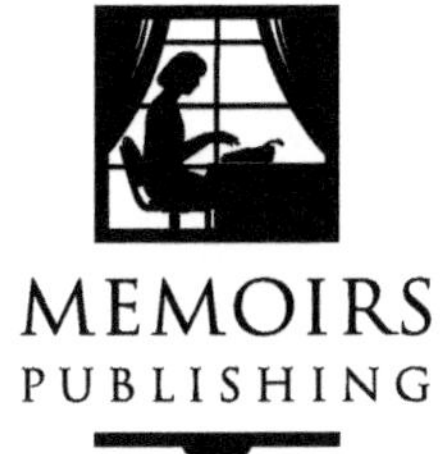

MEMOIRS
PUBLISHING

1A The Market Place Cirencester Gloucestershire GL7 2PR
info@memoirsbooks.co.uk | www.memoirspublishing.com

First published in England, 2013

Book jacket design Ray Lipscombe

ISBN 978-1-86151-151-5

Printed in England

ACKNOWLEDGEMENTS

For the historical material contained in this publication I have relied partly on a dissertation written by Margaret Purchase in May 1975 when she was a student at the Chorley Adult College of Education (today Lancashire College on Southport Road, Chorley). As far as I am aware this material was not published outside the college. Ms Purchase carried out taped interviews with the artist. I have been unable to contact her regarding this project.

I have also relied on my own 'Isherwood archives', which contain publicity for his exhibitions, photographs, press reports, numerous letters from the artist addressed to my family and the content of four audio cassettes, which I recorded with the artist in 1975, as well as my own notes. Much of the material contained in this publication has not been published previously.

I thank Frank Carey for allowing me to access his archive on Isherwood; Molly Isherwood; Merrilyn Guest; my wife Eileen and Gerry Fitzhenry for reading and correcting the manuscript and for encouraging me to complete this work; Karen Lawrinson for helping me to prepare the manuscript; and Geoffrey Shryhane for providing some notes. I thank Molly Isherwood (the Isherwood Estate) too for permission to reproduce plates of Isherwood's paintings. I also visited Tate Britain and the Museum of Wigan Life, which hold small archives on Isherwood.

I also draw the reader's attention to *Isherwood* by Stephen Eckersley, published as a limited edition of 250 copies by Vicarage Publishing in 2009, which contains a biography of Isherwood (see the update in the text). Together, these two biographies give the most complete description of the life and work of James Lawrence Isherwood published to date. They are intended to be complementary to each other.

PHOTOGRAPHS AND PLATES

Front cover: Mevagissey (1963; oil on board; 28 x 32cm).

James Lawrence Isherwood.

The Scarisbrick Hotel, Southport.

Houses of Parliament – Sunset (1975; oil on canvas; 45 x 65 cm).

Battersea Power Station (1975; oil on board; 30 x 40 cm).

69 Brookhouse Street, Wigan.

61 Darlington Street, Wigan.

151 Wigan Lane – 'Leywood' (the semi-detached house on the right).

Wigan and Leigh College.

Wigan All-Saints' Parish Church.

3 Northumberland Avenue, Trafalgar Square, now a Garfunkel's restaurant.

The Sherlock Holmes public house.

Left to right: Frank Carey, James Lawrence Isherwood and Douglas J Edwards (former Lord Mayor of Manchester) at the opening of the show at the University of Salford in 1975.

Professor Hans Suschitzky at the University of Salford show in 1975.

One of the weekend gatherings at the Scarisbrick Hotel.
Back row: Dr Brian Iddon, Bertie Dawson, Lou Fine (a record producer who worked with Hughie Green) and Tony Hale (Head of Music at Capitol Radio).
Front row: Marjorie and Frank Carey, Mrs Hale, Merrilyn Iddon and Mrs Fine (Picture by Graham Sherrif, Photographics, Southport).

Lady in Black (1975; oil on canvas; 50 x 60 cm).

Lady in Mink (1975; oil on canvas; 50 x 75 cm).

The Mirror (1975; pen and crayon on paper; 9 x 10 cm).

Wigan Red Sky (1975; oil on board; 9 x 15 cm).

Willows, Oxford (oil on board; 25 x 35 cm).

Roman Bath (1963; oil on board; 30 x 40 cm).

The Spanish Clown (1975; oil on board; 40 x 50 cm).

Guards at Buckingham Palace (1975; acrylic paint on canvas; 45 x 60 cm).

The Boat (1977; signed by Pat 'Isherwood', probably painted by Lawrence Isherwood; oil on board; 30 x 40 cm).

Devon Cottage (oil on board; 35 x 45 cm).

Wigan Stocking Factory (1962; oil on board; 45 x 60 cm).

The Isherwood family grave in Gidlow Cemetery, Wigan.

Molly and Gordon Isherwood at the opening of Wigan's History Shop in 1992.

Ian McCartney MP (Molly Isherwood on his right, her son Clive standing behind) at the opening of the show at Wigan Town Hall in 2002 (Eileen and Dr Brian Iddon are on the right of the picture and Fraser and Mandy White are standing behind Ian McCartney).

Mevagissey (1963; oil on board; 28 x 32 cm).

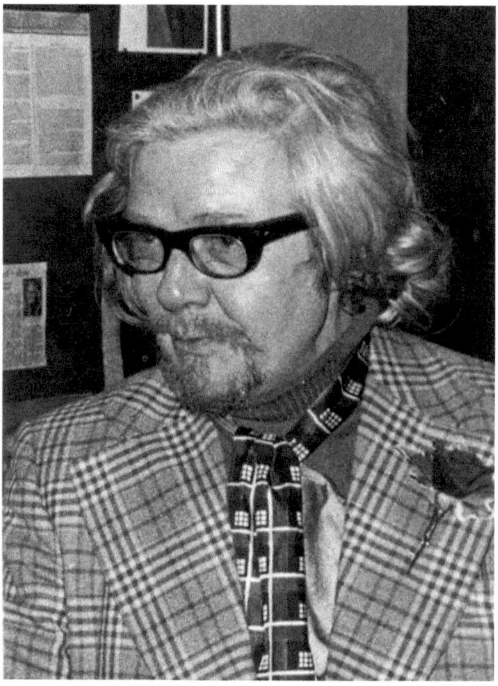

James Lawrence Isherwood

PROLOGUE

ISHERWOOD, THE CAREYS AND THE SCARISBRICK HOTEL

Frank Carey was born in Chorlton, Manchester and served for three years in the RAF as a ground crew member. He was attracted to work in the Midland Hotel in Manchester by talking to their staff, who visited the gentlemen's outfitters where he worked as a young man. It was during his time at the Midland Hotel that he became conscious of the perpetual need for hotels to hire staff from agencies, and he decided to set up a staff agency of his own.

Frank and Marjorie Carey's staff agency was supplying staff to the Scarisbrick Hotel in Southport for weddings and other busy events when the hotel fell on hard times, mainly through poor management, and its owners declared themselves bankrupt in 1972. Frank and Marjorie approached the main creditor, Scottish and Newcastle Breweries, who decided in March 1972 to appoint Frank Carey as manager of the hotel. Later, Frank and Marjorie became owners of the hotel. They worked very hard, the fortunes of the hotel were turned around and it became popular once again.

Isherwood walked into the Scarisbrick Hotel in 1972, just after the change of ownership. "We just sort of inherited Lawrence with the furniture and fittings" said Frank Carey. "He had a provisional booking for an exhibition at the hotel and wanted to be sure as new managers that we would go through with the arrangements. We did and soon became good friends." Isherwood had held exhibitions previously in Southport at the Imperial Hotel.

A word about how I came to know Isherwood and his work. My father, John (Jack) Iddon, was one of five brothers and two sisters who survived into adulthood from ten children born to Richard and Alice Iddon between 1892 and 1911 in Tarleton, then a small village on the West Lancashire Plain, midway between Preston, Ormskirk and Southport. In March 1975 I

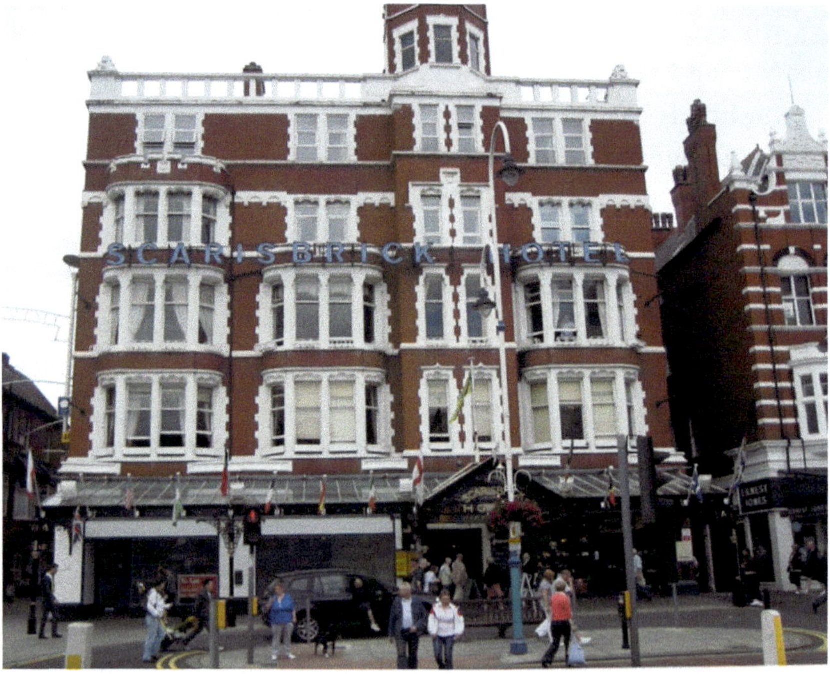

The Scarisbrick Hotel, Southport.

attended the funeral in Tarleton of my Uncle Dick (Richard Iddon), who died at the age of 73 on 12 March, the last of the five brothers to die. I felt so depressed after the funeral that I suggested to Merrilyn (my first wife) that we should go to Southport for a walk.

We parked on The Promenade and walked down Neville Street. As we turned right at the bottom of Neville Street into Lord Street, where the Kardomah Cafe used to be, I was attracted by three or four paintings in the window of a building society and a poster that was advertising an exhibition of paintings by James Lawrence Isherwood at the nearby Scarisbrick Hotel.

I recalled a conversation I had had with my University of Salford colleague Professor Hans Suschitzky, who had extolled the virtues of this particular artist, so we decided to visit the exhibition, which was held in the Derby Room on the first floor of the Scarisbrick Hotel. The 'Brick', with its eye-catching architecture and sixty bedrooms, stands in a prominent position almost opposite the civic buildings on Lord Street, facing Eastbank Street.

Isherwood's paintings, many unframed, were laid out on tables along the walls of the room and the artist was there to make the sales. We discovered that Isherwood had become a 'resident artist' in room 202, which overlooked Lord Street.

Merrilyn and I had several tours of the paintings and became engaged in conversation with Isherwood. We bought two oil paintings from him, one a view of Battersea Power Station across the River Thames from the embankment on the Pimlico side of the river and the other a view of the Houses of Parliament across the River Thames from the opposite embankment of the river (the South Bank). Twenty two years later I lived in

Pimlico's Dolphin Square, almost opposite Battersea power station, when I became a Member of Parliament in 1997. I still have the oil painting of the Houses of Parliament.

A piece on Isherwood appeared in the *Southport Visiter* on 6 March 1975 showing him painting 'The Houses of Parliament' (which he listed in the catalogue for the exhibition as 'Houses of Parliament – Sunset') in his room at the Scarisbrick Hotel. 'Battersea Power Station' was incorrectly listed as 'Chelsea Power Station' in the catalogue.

We spent over two and a half hours in the Scarisbrick Hotel that day. Isherwood introduced us to Frank Carey, who helped to rehabilitate him after a long period in C1 Psychiatric Ward at Billinge Hospital (now demolished and replaced with a housing development), which was close to Wigan, where he was treated for alcohol dependency and depression.

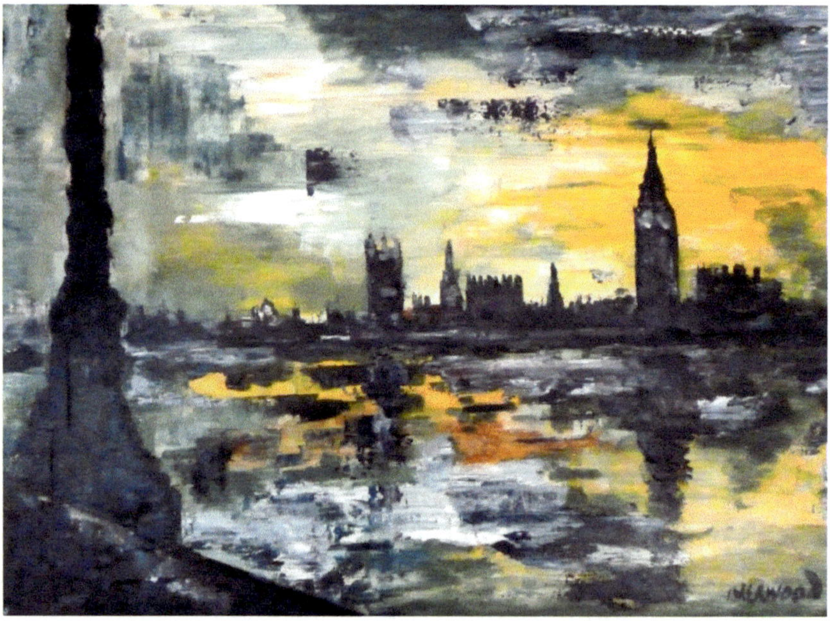

Houses of Parliament - Sunset (1975, oil on canvas; 45 x 65cm).

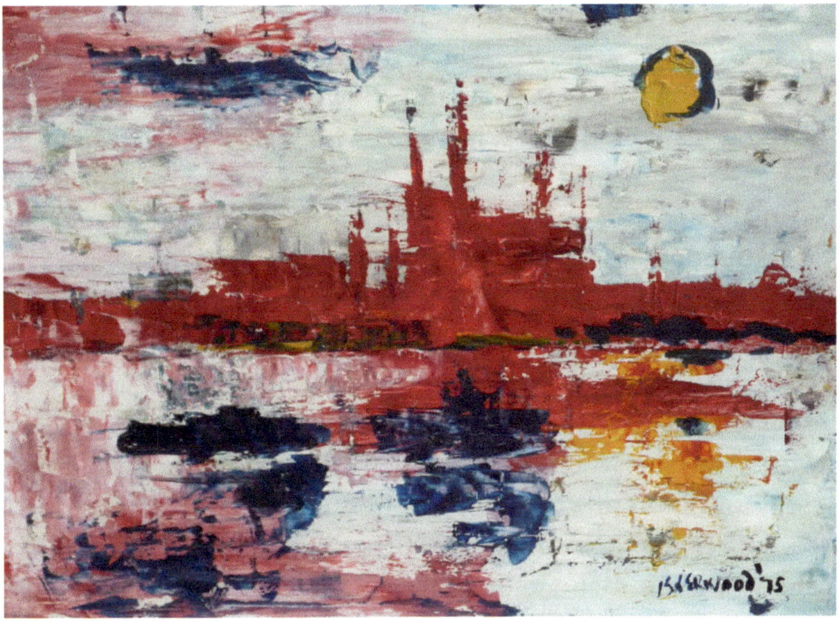

Battersea Power Station (1975; oil on board; 30 x 40cm).

That was the beginning of a close friendship between Lawrence and my family which, for me, lasted until the evening before Lawrence died.

Isherwood was 'Jim' to his closest friends, although I always called him Lawrence; he was 'Ishy' or Uncle Lawrence to my two young children, Sally and Sheena, aged 10 and 7 respectively in 1975.

THE ORIGINS OF THIS BOOK

When asked what I would do in retirement I told my family and friends that one of the first things I intended to do was to write a biography of James Lawrence Isherwood in an attempt to help grant him the recognition he had deserved when he was alive.

He never courted the art establishment; in general he hated agents/dealers, who he believed ripped him off with their excessive commissions. He had a 'down' too on the place of his birth, Wigan, and on Wiganers, who he believed failed to recognise his talents as an artist. Yet he yearned for recognition as an artist of some stature, especially from his own townsfolk.

I attended an exhibition of Isherwood paintings at the Mill House Gallery in the Old Windmill, Mill Lane, on the banks of the canal in Parbold on Saturday 10 October 2008. I wasn't able to get to the private view the evening before but it was an excellent collection of his paintings. I engaged the young gallery owner, an Isherwood enthusiast, in conversation and told him of my ambition to write a biography. I learned that two brothers from Leigh had been in the process of writing a book on Isherwood but that one of them had died suddenly. I explained that, if I could help in any way to get the book out, I would offer my services to the surviving brother.

On 11 June 2009 an email arrived to invite Eileen and me to attend the launch of a limited edition (sadly, only 250 copies were published) of a book on Isherwood by Stephen Eckersley.[1] It is dedicated to his brother, Vincent Eckersley (1939-2007), a photographer who produced most of the excellent artwork and photographs and designed 90% of the lay-out for the book before he died. The launch, which Eileen and I attended on Friday 3 July 2009, was held at The Room Four conference venue in Golborne. My copy of the book, which is number 41, was signed at the launch by Stephen Eckersley, Geoffrey Shryhane (a journalist with the *Wigan Observer*), Molly (Isherwood's sister-in-law) and Clive Isherwood (Molly's son).

Isherwood is an impressive book. However, the author admits that there may be gaps in it, and there are. So, I decided to tell my own story about life with Isherwood, to paint a picture of him as I saw him. My biography is intended to be complementary to the Eckersley[1] biography and includes a lot of unpublished material relating to the period 1975-1989.

JAMES LAWRENCE ISHERWOOD

ISHERWOOD'S EARLY YEARS

Lawrence's grandfather, John Henry Isherwood (born on 10 October 1852), arrived in Wigan from the Wirral as a hatter and opened a shop in the old arcade. Wigan was where he met his wife Alice (born 1851, maiden name Rider or Ryder), also a hatter. Alice's family had a shop and lived in Harrogate Street, Wigan. A photograph taken in 1860 showing the Isherwood hatter's shop in the arcade hung in the Turnkey Restaurant in King Street for many years. Lawrence's paternal grandfather worked hard to establish his business and invested his profits in property.

Lawrence's father Henry Lawrence Isherwood (he was called Harry) (born 1888) married Lily Leyland (born 1891; the family were from Denton) at Wigan All Saints' Parish Church in the summer of 1915, and they began their married life at 69 Brookhouse Street in Scholes, a part of the hilly district of Whelley on the Bolton side of Wigan. The wedding was an expensive affair.

Lily was the daughter of James Leyland (born 1867) and his wife Sarah Catherine (born 1867, maiden name Grindrod). The couple were shoemakers who lived at 8 Greenough Street, where Harry was employed as a cobbler before he fell in love with Lily. As the Leyland family grew in

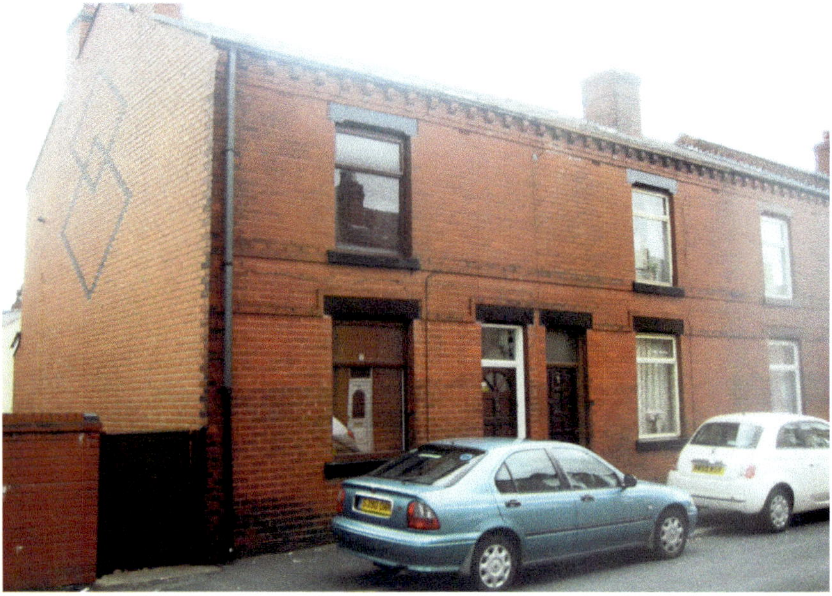

69 Brookhouse Street, Scholes.

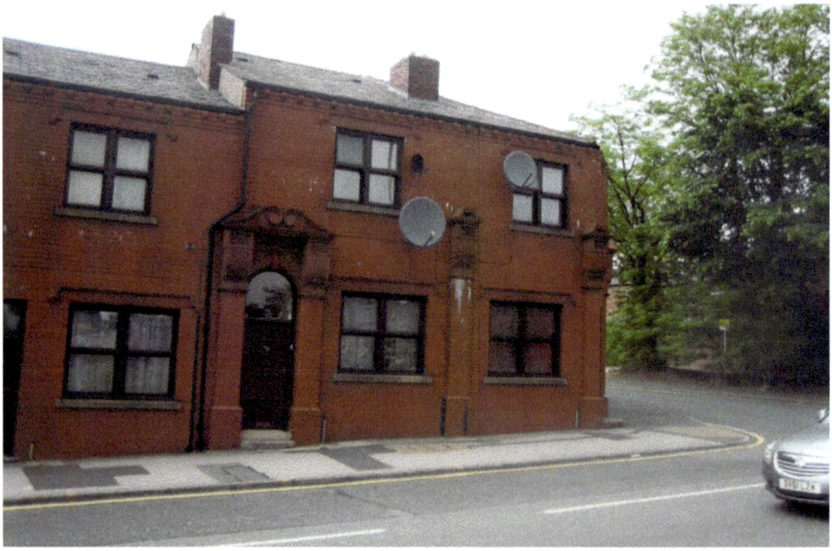

61 Darlington Street, Wigan.

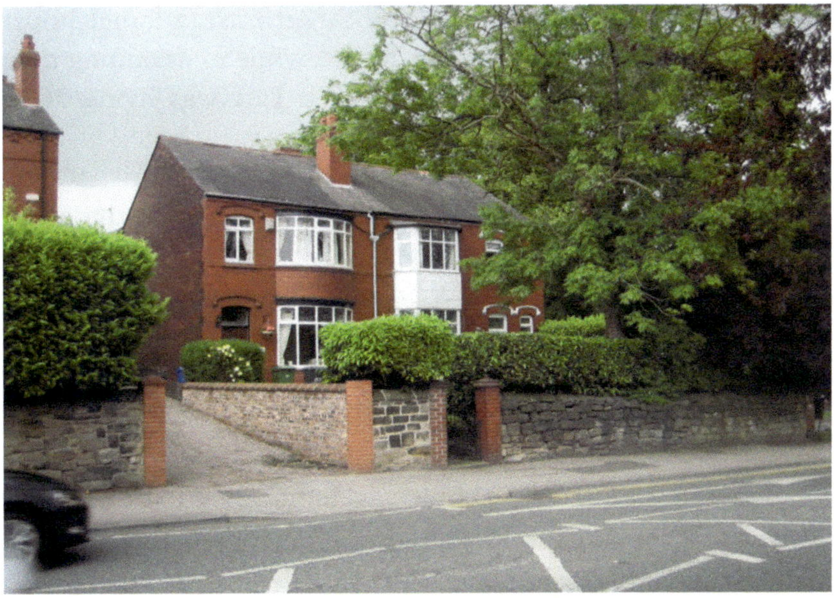

151 Wigan Road - 'Leywood' (the semi-detached house on the right).

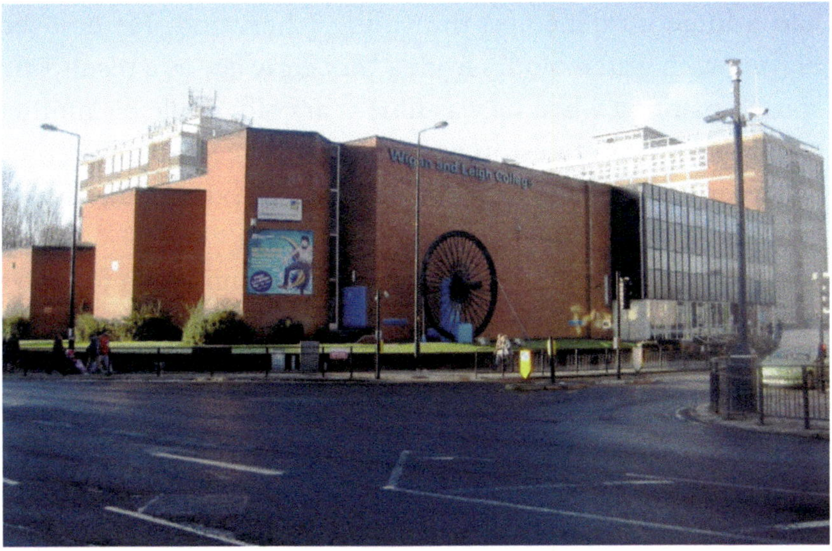

Wigan and Leigh College [2].

size they moved to 61 Darlington Street East, a larger house on the corner with Brookhouse Street, while maintaining their shoe business at 8 Greenough Street. Lily was living at 61 Darlington Street when she married Harry.

James Lawrence Isherwood was born on 7 April 1917 in Brookhouse Street while his father was serving in the army. Lawrence's brother Gordon Leyland Isherwood was born in Darlington Street in 1920. Whenever Lawrence and I travelled into Wigan by car through Scholes he would point to where these houses stood. The entertainer George Formby was born George Hoy Booth at 3 Westminster Street, Scholes.

Lawrence attended the New Jerusalem Primary School in Warrington Road (the building was demolished to build a Lidl supermarket), just round the corner from his home. Mother Lily showed Lawrence the colours of the silk and cotton threads she used for her embroidery and insisted that he remember the names of the colours she showed him, which had a huge influence on the young Isherwood. He enjoyed playing with watercolours from a very early age as a result, and started painting when he was nine years old. While his mother encouraged his interest in art, the general feeling at that time was that art was not for boys. In any case the family had a business to run.

At the age of 11 Lawrence passed an examination for entry into Whelley Secondary Modern School, where he was one of the first pupils in 1928. In 1929 the family moved to 151 Wigan Lane, a newly-built house which was named 'Leywood', an amalgamation of the Leyland and Isherwood family names. This pre-war semi-detached house was built to last with Accrington brick, and still stands today opposite the Royal Albert Edward Infirmary (Wigan Infirmary) and next to the Bellingham Hotel on the A49. A granite plaque has been provided by the Isherwood family, which is fitted to the front of the house to remind people that it is the house in which James Lawrence Isherwood lived and painted.

Lawrence was a bright pupil at school where, at the age of 13, he entered the commercial course a year ahead of most pupils. He studied French, bookkeeping, shorthand and typing and passed the examinations which would allow him to continue his studies at Wigan Mining and Technical School (today Wigan and Leigh College[2]). Instead of leaving secondary school at the age of 14 the Headmaster employed him at the rate of one shilling (5p) a week as an unofficial secretary. As part of his duties he typed examination papers. As a loner he mixed little with fellow pupils and the Headmaster trusted him not to pass on the contents of these papers to the students.

He was then offered two jobs, one at the auctioneers Hendersons at the rate of 7s 6d (37.5p) a week and the other as an office boy at Brown and Haigh, a clothing manufacturer, at the rate of 12s 6d (62.5p) a week. He accepted the higher paid job and continued his studies at Wigan Mining and Technical School in the evenings. Although he was given a small ledger of his own in recognition of his ability, Lawrence hated office work.

At the age of 17 Lawrence started a romantic relationship with Kay Winstanley, who lived at 5 Upper Dickinson Street. He met her just after his grandfather John Henry Isherwood died in 1936 when she was 14. Isherwood painted a watercolour of London Bridge in her autograph book at this time but it doesn't appear to have survived.

In 1937, at the age of 20, Isherwood started work at Winstanley's jewellery business at 29 Market Street, which was owned by Kay's father. Because he was regularly late for work Mr Winstanley gave him a gold wrist-watch for his 21st birthday with the comment "hope this helps you keep better time". The wrist-watch is today in the ownership of Molly Isherwood, Lawrence's sister-in-law.

Isherwood survived working in the shop for about two years but was sacked by Mr Winstanley because he mowed the lawn at home rather than turn in for work on one of the busiest days of the working week – a Saturday afternoon – which Lawrence believed to be his afternoon off. Lawrence abandoned his romance with Kay Winstanley as a result.

Whilst at Wigan Mining and Technical School he decided to enrol on an art course. He had taken an interest in photographs of London and began drawing sketches of the city as a result. As the only student in his year on the art course at the Technical School he was taught subjects by Mr Hewells which he did not really appreciate, etching and black and white drawing, for example. He was expected to draw a bust of Socrates and develop an eye for the shading that he observed. He was not introduced to work in oils.

The rebel in him was beginning to show. He wanted to develop his own style of art and not be bound by convention. One of his regrets later, however, was that he never kept the work he did at Wigan Mining and Technical School, so there is no record of his early work. Isherwood attended art classes at the 'Tech' in the 1930s, probably between 1934 and 1939, although different dates are quoted in the different brief biographies of his life that have been published.

In his late teenage years his interest in painting watercolours increased. He was a founding member of Wigan Art Society in 1952 (or 1955 - he gave different dates in two biographies) and became a member of Bolton Art Circle, Blackburn Artists' Society, Blackpool and Fylde Art Society and Manchester Art Club as well. He observed that their members all painted in the same style and that being innovative was frowned upon. His early attempts to exhibit his watercolours were not very successful; he preferred to exhibit in the Spring Exhibitions at the Harris Art Gallery in Preston.

In his youth one of Isherwood's hobbies was rowing, for which he won a trophy; the other he listed as stamp collecting. He told me that he rowed on the Leeds and Liverpool canal at Haigh, near Wigan.

When the war started the Isherwood brothers volunteered for service. Gordon joined the RAF and served for six years (he was stationed in Wales) but Lawrence was rejected by the RAF because of poor eyesight. Life in the army in the Pioneer Corps (Lawrence was stationed in Liverpool from 1940 to 1941) was not for him; he developed symptoms of anxiety and tension and could not cope with the expected discipline of army life. He was discharged, diagnosed with neurasthenia.

The Isherwood family business at this time was making and selling shoes. Their shop, Leylands, was badly damaged by bombing in 1940, but Harry Isherwood managed to re-establish himself and carry on with his trade. Lawrence was persuaded to join his father to build up their business again at 8 Greenough Street, but his heart wasn't in his work and, much to the disappointment of his father, his attendance at the shop was irregular. These premises were demolished in 1968 and Greenough Street was widened and redeveloped.

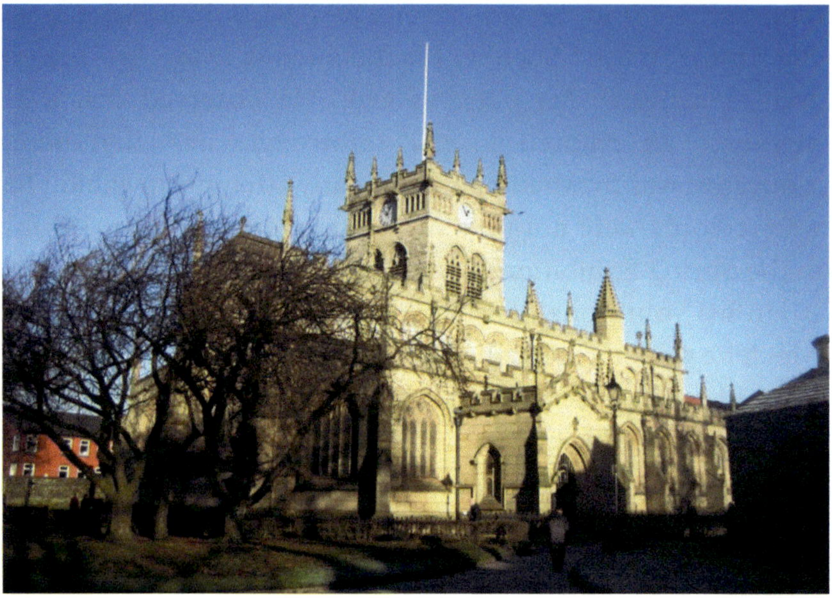

Wigan All-Saints' Parish Church.

A DOUBLE WEDDING

Lawrence attended dances at Wigan Mining and Technical School, where he set eyes on his future wife, Florence Banks, a hairdresser who owned her own business, Pemberton Hollins Salon. Although he was greatly attracted to her, he was too shy to make an approach to date her until one evening after he had been out drinking with his friends. They dared Lawrence to ask her out and within twelve months they were married.

In fact Lawrence and his brother Gordon married two sisters, on the same day. Lawrence Isherwood was 27 and Gordon 25 when they married Florence (19) and Mary (known as Molly), who was 17, on 28 June 1944. The sisters lived previously with their parents at 617 Ormskirk Road, Pemberton; their father Richard Banks was a taxi and funeral director. It was the first double wedding at Wigan All Saints' Parish Church. A red carpet was rolled out to receive all those who attended. Surprisingly, Gordon and Lawrence's parents did not attend this special wedding; they believed that because Lawrence wasn't earning any money at the time he would not be able to support Florence.

Gordon found a flat in a large house on Wigan Lane, which he rented for three guineas a week, and the foursome lived together there for about six months. When the owner's son married a Russian princess and returned home they had to leave the flat, and Lawrence and Florence decided to live with Harry and Lily Isherwood at 151 Wigan Lane. Florence and Molly found it difficult to call Lily Isherwood 'mother', so Lily suggested that they call her 'Mother Lily' instead, a title that was reflected later in Isherwood's paintings of her.

Lawrence would paint until the early hours of the morning, a lifestyle that was not conducive to keeping a marriage together. He still was not selling any of his paintings. When the owner of the hairdressing business at 57 Darlington Street, where Florence worked after she was married, offered Florence the business for £100, Lawrence's grandmother lent her the money to purchase it, and she became self-employed.

One day Florence came home and told Lawrence that she had been offered the keys to another shop with accommodation in Wallgate for a rent of 35s (£1.75p) a week, but Lawrence refused to move. He wanted to continue to live with his parents, a situation that had created tensions between himself and Florence. Lawrence told Florence to take the house and live in it herself, and she decided to leave him. Florence moved to a rented property in Brookhouse Street while continuing to run her business at 57 Darlington Street. Lawrence continued to see her, but they slowly drifted apart.

Although the marriage only lasted eighteen months divorce was not granted until 1951. Florence met Frank, a lecturer, and they left Wigan eighteen months later to live in Wiltshire.

In 1940 Lawrence decided to buy some oil paints as he was passing Wildings art shop. I had not seen his first picture in oils, 'Wigan Pier', painted later, in 1951, until the launch of Stephen Eckersley's book on Isherwood. It is now in Stephen's private collection and is reproduced in the book *Isherwood.* Isherwood painted Wigan Pier several times. His earliest known watercolour of it, painted in 1932, was reproduced as a postcard in 1958.

Isherwood began selling his paintings in the window of the family shoe business in Greenough Street, where he also painted. At that time a pair of ladies' shoes cost about 19s11d (99p). Lawrence's paintings were advertised at £4 but just as his father was willing to take payment for shoes in instalments, the paintings could also be paid for 'on tick'.

As a founding member of Wigan Art Society, Isherwood's first real exhibition was on 4 November 1952 at the Rotary Club's Hobbies Exhibition in Wigan Drill Hall, where his paintings were displayed along with those of other members of the Art Society.

ISHERWOOD'S FIRST ONE-MAN EXHIBITION

In an interview in 1975, Isherwood told Margaret Purchase that his first one-man exhibition had been held in the Balcarres Arms public house, probably the one in Greenough Street (see note[3] in the Appendix), but in an interview he gave to the *Southport Visiter* (published on 4 July 1982) he told the journalist that his first one-man show was in the Bricklayer's

Arms in Wigan in 1952, which is probably correct. Isherwood's paintings were hung around the bar and a poster was displayed outside announcing 'Art to the Public – Exhibition of Paintings'. The exhibition was a success. However, Isherwood did not regard himself as a professional artist at this stage in his life. He continued to sell his paintings from the shop window of his father's business.

On his 37th birthday he held another exhibition in the Minorca Hotel in Wallgate, Wigan, but in an upstairs room. Those taking their drinks downstairs were reluctant to go upstairs to view the paintings and the show was a failure. Isherwood told the story of his mother Lily refusing to let him transport the paintings to the Minorca in the family car, so in a fit of defiance he took them there in a borrowed wheelbarrow instead.

At the Minorca Hotel he sold a painting entitled 'All this and Everest too', a 30" x 45" composite painting of the Queen's Coronation, for an offer of £5, which led to a headline in the *Daily Express*. Later he very much regretted selling that painting for such a low price.

THE ROYAL OAK HOTEL, CHORLEY

His fourth one-man show (he might have put on a show before this one in the Bowling Green Hotel in Wigan Lane) was at the Royal Oak on the A6 in Chorley town centre. It opened on 21 September 1954 and ran for one month; it was more successful than his earlier shows.

The Royal Oak was a residential hotel, with people staying there from the other parts of Britain, and some of them had an interest in paintings. The exhibition was better organised,

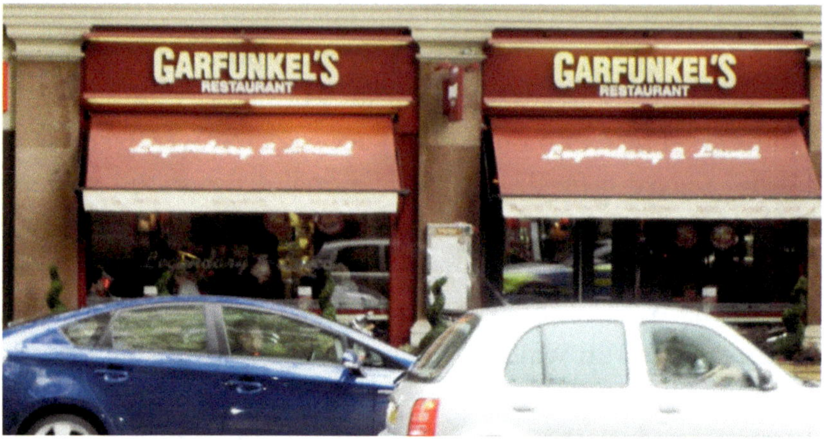

3 Northumberland Avenue, Trafalgar Square, now a Garfunkel's restaurant.

too. The local road builder Leonard Fairclough JP opened it and Isherwood paid for a finger buffet and drinks. This was the only exhibition of his paintings Isherwood's father ever attended. Mother Lily understood Isherwood's need to paint, but the rest of the family could never understand why he didn't take his father's business seriously; at the very least, it would have provided him with a steady income.

In Chorley a visitor to his exhibition told him about the Coffee House at 3 Northumberland Avenue, Trafalgar Square in London, which later became the Fontainebleau Coffee House (today it is a branch of Garfunkel's Restaurants). The owners encouraged new artists, but only after a recommendation or a visit by one of their representatives or contacts to an exhibition by the artist. The Chorley contact took some of Isherwood's paintings to show the owners of the Coffee House, who decided to put on an exhibition there the following April, in 1955.

The next show after Chorley was at the Springfield Hotel

in December 1954, back in Wigan. In the programme for his '15th One-Man Show', held at Warrington Art Gallery between 12 December 1956 and 5 January 1957, with 50 paintings on display, Isherwood wrote:

> "NOTE! On Dec 19 at 7 pm Mr J R Rimmer, BEM AMA, Director of the Gallery will sit when Mr Isherwood gives a portrait demo. in oils, and lectures. Everyone welcome". That was followed by "Commission for portraits in oils accepted: 25 gns."

ISHERWOOD BECOMES RECOGNISED

Isherwood's career as an artist took off in the 1950s. He realised that an artist has to paint paintings people want to buy, and he developed a number of popular themes which he painted over and over again. London scenes, horse racing, the industrial landscape (especially in Wigan), including pits, miners and pit brow lassies, clowns, self portraits, portraits of famous people such as 'Monty' (Viscount Montgomery of Alamein), Sir Francis Chichester and Gandhi, seascapes, nudes and, later, paintings based on his travels abroad are common amongst his prolific output of paintings.

Isherwood realised too that paintings sell better when the artist courts publicity. He began to make contacts in the local and national media. He often sold unframed paintings from table tops or at the roadside, but he also knew that framed paintings sold better. When I knew him he would often buy a 'job lot' of cheap frames and make the hardboard on which he painted his oils fit the frames. I remember taking him to pick up some cheap frames from Northern Frames at a workshop near Victoria Station in Manchester. He would spend a few hours applying white paint to the boards before he began to paint a picture on them. Painting on canvas was a luxury for Isherwood.

Isherwood always sought recognition rather than riches. He often gave away paintings or exchanged them for favours or even fines after he had been stopped by the police.

Isherwood was always proud to be a Fellow of the Royal Society of Arts (FRSA), but his first application in 1950 was refused. He acquired this title in 1955 and proudly announced it at a one-man show, his twelfth, held at the Swan Hotel in Bolton, which ran from 24 July until 18 August 1956. The show was opened by Mr J R Rimmer, Director of the Warrington Art Gallery, who also opened another Isherwood exhibition, his sixteenth, held for "an indefinite period" at the Legh House Restaurant in Warrington. Isherwood was also awarded Life Fellowship of the International Society of Arts and Letters (FIAL), Switzerland in 1959 for 'notable achievements in art' and the Silver Medal of the Italian Academy, Rome in 1970.

Isherwood listed himself as a cartoonist with the *Manchester Evening News* from 1951-1955 and as an 'extras' actor with Granada TV from 1955-1960. Once he proudly showed me his Equity card. For a biography that he constructed for the *International Book of Honour*, published in 1984, he reported that he had taught at the Chorley Private School and operated the 'Isherwood 6d School of Oil Painting for Children' in 1955 at the Greenough Street cobbler's shop.

Other artists began to take an interest in his paintings. Ruskin Spear visited a joint exhibition of his work with the work of other new and unknown artists that was mounted at the Midday Studios in Manchester. Spear judged most of the works on exhibition there as “a load of rubbish, except that one... which has style, vitality, and everything a picture should have”. It was a painting of a young girl that Isherwood had prepared for the exhibition. He was being noticed by influential people at last.

ISHERWOOD LOSES HIS FATHER

Isherwood was proud of his family and the crafts they had been engaged in and learned how to turn and stitch shoes. The first finishing machine for shoes ever to be used in Wigan was installed in Leylands, the shop in Greenough Street, which opened in 1887. It attracted such a lot of attention that people used to stand outside the shop to watch the Isherwoods finishing shoes; previously they had done this by hand on the first floor of their shop. The machine was later donated to the Municipal Museum in Wigan.

Isherwood’s father suffered from angina for over twenty years. On 25 April 1955 Harry felt so ill that he decided to ask the doctor to call. His surgery was next door - where the Bellingham Hotel stands today. After waiting all day and watching the doctor drive past the Isherwood home several times, Harry got out of his chair crying “Oh, beggar the doctor” and told Lily that he was going down Wigan Lane, probably to the Saracen’s Head public house, to pay a bill for a crate of beer that they had delivered to his home. Some nurses waiting at the bus stop in front of the house saw Harry lurching up Wigan Lane on his return and hesitate as he approached 'Leywood'. He staggered against the front garden wall and collapsed on the front gate, which gave way and precipitated Harry onto the ground just as a bus stopped at the bus stop. The bus driver carried Harry Isherwood back to the house, but he was dead. He was 67 years old.

Later Lily said "He never kissed me when he left. He was so annoyed with the doctor that he just went out".

Lawrence was mending shoes at the shop in Greenough Street when a hairdresser from a nearby shop came in to inform him that he was needed at home urgently. Lawrence cycled home and found his father sitting in his favourite chair, still wearing his boots but dead. When someone from the infirmary came across to remove the body, Lily said, "No, you're not touching him, it's too late".

This was a turning point in Lawrence's life; his father's early death taught him that life can be short and that opportunities have to be grasped when they present themselves. He decided from that moment on to concentrate on his painting. "Blow the shop, blow the people and blow Lancashire" commented Isherwood. "Do what you want and do it properly."

The Leylands' shoe business closed at 8 Greenough Street after that.

After leaving the RAF at the age of 31 Gordon Isherwood established himself in a shoe business at 61 Darlington Street where he was born, two doors away from Florence's hairdressing business at number 57. Later he acquired a second shop at 53 Wallgate, Wigan. In April 1955 Gordon and Molly were about to move into their newly-built home in Appley Bridge and Gordon's father Harry was due to travel the short distance out of Wigan on the A49 to see it. Sadly, Harry never made the journey.

THE COFFEE HOUSE, 3 NORTHUMBERLAND AVENUE, WESTMINSTER

Lawrence and Mother Lily travelled together to the Coffee House in Northumberland Avenue, Westminster, London in April 1955. They made enough money to cover their expenses but did not enjoy what the art critics had to say about Lawrence's paintings. After his first exhibition at the Coffee House, Isherwood had one exhibition a year there until it closed in 1967, shortly after its change of name to the Fontainebleau, when it became a restaurant.

The influential art critic Mervyn Levy opened his third show at the Coffee House on 13 May 1957 (Isherwood's seventeenth one-man show). In the programme Isherwood wrote: "During 1957 Mr Isherwood will take Art to the Motorists all over Great Britain by holding roadside art exhibitions and open-air shows."

Mervyn Levy wrote of the show in the *Art News and Review* on 25 May 1957:

> "Mr Lawrence Isherwood, a Northerner, is a painter of considerable energy, working, often with consummate brilliance, in the established Expressionist tradition. For him, the swift, unimpeded flow of paint from the fiery mouths of his brushes is a corollary of breathing; painting is the logical extension, a supplement of being, and as natural. Paint or die, his pictures seem to say. It is his passionate vitality that makes such an engaging and stimulating artist. One is affected, deeply, by

the pulse and movement, the pure rhythm and restless dynamic of his work. His subjects range from black stockinged women of the North (he lives and works in Wigan) wrapped in the clouds of their fringed shawls, to fresh, glittering, sea breezy shots of St. Ives, bursting with the fresh light of the nostril tickling coast. He renders flower subjects too, with an ease, and power of simplification, that is completely satisfying.

'Lancashire Madonna' is perhaps his most striking work. A painting of his mother, shawled, and with clasped hands, not a bit sentimentalised, and symbolising all the sensible, average mothers of the world. For she is not only a symbol, but also one feels, a woman who has enjoyed and endured the miracle of life, with simple resignation, and a modicum of wisdom. The wisdom that comes to the Madonna who has borne children, yet retained, in spite of knowledge, the purity of sheer innocence. A sort of Madonna Superior. It is painted with a nervous and devouring excitement that trembles visibly in the flesh of paint, the canvas irradiating the devotion so evidently felt by the artist.

"Mr Isherwood is unquestionably an artist of talent and, carefully selected, he would I am sure, be shown to profitable advantage in a West End gallery. Meanwhile, congratulations to the Coffee House for putting him on in the first place."

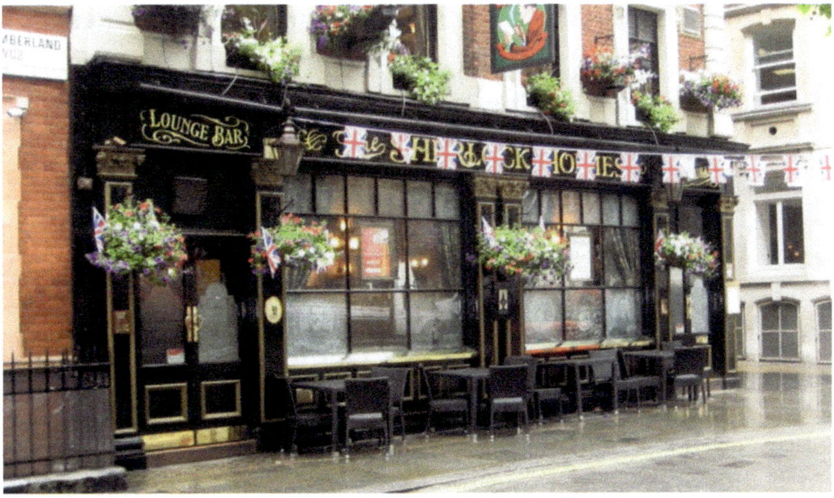

The Sherlock Holmes public house.

Mother Lily and Lawrence enjoyed meeting the great and the good in London. He sold one of his paintings to Colonel Alfred D Wintle of the War Office, who said, "What I like about Isherwood's paintings is at least you know which way to hang them".

Wintle was, like Isherwood, an eccentric but with a distinguished military career, which is related in Stephen Eckersley's book *Isherwood.*

In 1960, Sir Albert Richardson, President of the Royal Academy, opened his fifth show at the Coffee House and was very complimentary about Isherwood's paintings: "He captures everything so quickly and in an imitable way that I envy."

Mother Lily and son frequented the Sherlock Holmes public house (just off Northumberland Avenue at the junction of Northumberland Street and Craven Passage) where they met quite a few famous people. Isherwood recalled that they met the actor Richard Briers in 1967, then appearing in *The*

Bells at the Playhouse Theatre. Molly and Gordon Isherwood occasionally accompanied Lawrence and Mother Lily on their London trips, where they would see West End shows such as *Mame*, starring Ginger Rogers (it opened for a short season in the West End in 1969).

SOUTHPORT

Isherwood held exhibitions in October/November at the Imperial Hotel in Southport in 1956 (his fourteenth one-man show, at the age of 39), 1958 (his twenty-eighth) and 1961 (his fifty-fourth). Local or national politicians opened these shows. The 1958 show, for example, was opened by Col. R Fleetwood-Hesketh, Member of Parliament for Southport. 'Tommy Steele with Two Heads' (see later) was advertised for 110 guineas in the catalogue.

At the 1956 Imperial Hotel exhibition, framed prints of Wigan Pier were on sale for 7s 6d and Isherwood displayed some wire and plaster models which had provoked someone at an earlier Wigan exhibition to 'smash [them] up'. Isherwood repaired them, but they were 'stolen' from a later show in Liverpool, 'disfigured' at a show in London and 'threatened' at shows in Manchester and Bolton. Isherwood used these 'events' in his publicity materials.

Lawrence painted - and his mother is reported to have kept - a catalogue of every exhibition that they put on together and kept copies of the posters and the flyers prepared for each show. Sadly, a complete list of Isherwood's 'exhibitions' does not appear to exist today. Although he reported before he died that he had had nearly 300 'exhibitions', many of these were not the kind of exhibitions that established artists usually organise. He often sent copies of the posters and catalogues for his exhibitions and the press coverage of his work to those who he knew and to the Tate Gallery in London. The Museum of Wigan Life, at the junction of Rodney Street and Library Street in Wigan, has a small collection of his posters and catalogues.

Lawrence and Mother Lily travelled together across Britain, often holding roadside shows of Isherwood's paintings. They continued to show too in other unconventional venues, especially in public houses and the lay-bys of busy roads, such as the East Lancashire Road (A580), and they had one pavement show beneath the statue of Boadicea on Westminster Bridge, London.

A Cambridge University student purchased a painting at an exhibition held in the Bowling Green Hotel in Wigan Lane and invited Lawrence to put on a show at the university. Partly because Lawrence believed that he would not sell many paintings at good prices to students, but mainly because he was preparing for the show in London that was opened by Sir Albert Richardson, he refused this invitation. They had a show in Torquay planned as well.

1960: ISHERWOOD CRASHES HIS VAN

When Lawrence and his mother were driving back to Wigan from Torquay in 1960 in their red van they were involved in a serious accident near Madeley in Shropshire. Mother Lily was flung through the windscreen, which slashed her face and caused serious head injuries. Lawrence sustained injuries to his chest and ribs. The van was a write-off.

Mother Lily refused to be admitted to hospital and, as soon as her lacerated face had been sutured, they found accommodation in a cottage to recover overnight before travelling home with Gordon Isherwood the following evening. Despite her injuries Mother Lily insisted on being taken straight home; she refused to seek medical help, even when she arrived in Wigan.

When Molly Isherwood saw a bleeding ear the following day she took Mother Lily across the road to Wigan Infirmary to be examined. Lily had also suffered a split tongue, which left a scar for the rest of her days. She was in bed for six months at home following the accident and Lawrence said that she never recovered fully from it.

Isherwood attempted to cancel an exhibition he was preparing to mount at the Av Guard Gallery at 34a Brazenose Street, Manchester. However, the proprietor visited Isherwood at home to look at his paintings and decided that there were enough paintings in existence to put on the show, which went ahead on 30 August 1960 and ran until 17 September, with 40 oils on display. It was opened by Mrs Mullings, an agent for the Midday Studios in Manchester, and was well attended.

One of the visitors to this exhibition was L S Lowry, who bought an Isherwood entitled 'Minnie Small with Kitten' (also known as 'Shawled Woman and Cat') for £5 and declared an interest in Isherwood's work. "I only buy pictures I like and I bought an Isherwood years ago", Lowry said long after his purchase. He displayed Isherwood's picture in his studio.

THE CAMBRIDGE AND OXFORD COLLEGES

In 1961 the Isherwoods finally travelled to Cambridge University, where they mounted an exhibition in Downing College. Lawrence had been wrong about not selling his paintings there. The students, especially postgraduates who were buying their first paintings, bought anything and everything.

Queues of people were snapping up paintings that were on offer for £3 and £4. In two days the Isherwoods made £130.

After the success of their first exhibition in Cambridge, Lawrence returned with his mother several times. In 1970, for example, they visited Emmanuel College on 3-4 June, Corpus Christi College (Old Court) on 5-7 June, Christ's College on 8-10 June and Peterhouse College on 11-13 June. Exhibitions were also held on other occasions at St Catharine's, Newnham, Maudling, Downing, Magdalene, Caius, Corpus Christi, Churchill and Pembroke Colleges and in the famous Red Room at New College in Oxford, as well as in other colleges at Oxford University – Exeter, Lincoln, Magdalen, Oriel and Keble Colleges included. Prince Charles, the Prince of Wales, purchased a seascape from Isherwood when he was a student at Trinity College, Cambridge University.

In 1965 an Isherwood sold for $7,000 at the Palace Hotel in Las Vegas. Isherwood turned down an invitation to put on an exhibition in the USA.

THE IMPORTANCE OF MOTHER LILY IN ISHERWOOD'S LIFE

All the travelling – seventeen years of it - by the Isherwoods, in addition to the 1960 accident, was beginning to take its toll on Mother Lily, who was walking badly and generally weakening physically. Her memory started to deteriorate as well. Lawrence increasingly cared for her. He cooked and washed for her and encouraged her to keep going. He knew that without his mother, he would be lost. They had been very happy travelling together. They often sat either side of the fire with a drink in their hands, watching television. Lily liked gin, but Lawrence preferred to drink whisky.

Although Lawrence often gave people the impression that they had very little to do with his brother Gordon and his wife, Molly insists that this was not the case. Gordon and Molly would call on their way home from work and Lawrence and Mother Lily often went to Appley Bridge for tea on Sundays. They would spend Christmas day with Gordon and Molly, who visited 151 Wigan Lane on New Year's Day.

Mother Lily was the dominant character in her relationship with Lawrence, often treating him as she had when he had been a child, scolding him when she didn't approve of what he had done. She would throw things at him when she got really angry with him. Lily certainly didn't appreciate Lawrence painting nudes. Once, when he had taken a woman home to paint in the nude, she refused to allow her to pose.

Isherwood was certainly a charmer of women; I have seen him in action several times. Offering to paint a woman in the nude was a method of seduction for him, although it didn't always work. He painted more nudes after Mother Lily passed away than before, Lancashire nudes, Aberystwyth nudes, Southport nudes and college nudes. Wherever he went he tried to paint a nude. At the age of 60 he claimed to have given up sex, but he still went around saying to women who he hardly knew, "I'm past it now but, if you want, you can take your clothes off and I will give you a good painting". I have never been attracted to his paintings of nudes.

Lawrence told me a story about advertising for nudes to paint in the *Southport Visiter* but, when the newspaper made it a front-page story instead, he received requests from seventeen women to be painted in the nude.

Lily was reluctant to allow callers at 151 Wigan Lane into the home, although a local journalist, Geoffrey Shryhane of the *Wigan Observer*, who later became Isherwood's agent for a short period, was allowed in.

Mother and son enjoyed the cinema so much that they often went more than once a week. Thursday was their favourite day for the cinema. Lawrence would make his mother walk the two miles there and back for exercise in order to keep her mobile. He was afraid of losing her.

At his sixty-fifth exhibition, held from 28 April to 25 May 1963 at the Fontainebleau (previously the Coffee House) at 3 Northumberland Avenue in London, Isherwood used a quotation from an article written by John Robinson in the *Lancashire Evening Post*:

> "This year, Isherwood introduces his 'ATMOSPHERIC' oil paintings. It is a new technique which includes rain, sun, smoke and age, etc. - putting in the ATMOSPHERE of a subject rather than the details – executed in a technique which calls for careful control of paint that is allowed to flow in certain directions over the canvas."

Isherwood's hundredth one-man exhibition, and his last at the Fontainebleau, was held between 23 April and 4 June 1967; he was 50 on 7 April 1967 and Mother Lily had turned 75 that March. The catalogue listed 25 paintings, including a nude of Vanessa Redgrave.

By Christmas 1970 Mother Lily had "seized up" and was in bed until January 1971. She didn't want to get out of bed and walk and was in very poor health until a doctor suggested that she be admitted to Billinge Hospital for a few days for some tests. She was diagnosed to be suffering from diabetes, which they successfully treated. The doctors also discovered that Lily had an abscess on her womb and recommended a hysterectomy operation. Her son Gordon and his wife Molly thought Lily should go ahead with the operation, although Lawrence was conscious of what she had said to him as he carried her downstairs on her way to hospital on 4 February 1971: "Aye, it's all right going to hospital, but it's whether you come back or not." She made the same remark to Molly, who had seen blood on Mother Lily's slippers a few days previously.

Lily's condition deteriorated rapidly and Lawrence sat constantly with her, as did Gordon and Molly and their son Clive. Lawrence was filled with a mixture of grief and guilt. Lily died on 24 July 1971, aged 79.

Lawrence often told the story that there was a freak hailstorm that day with dark thunderclouds. He claims to have seen her face in those clouds as the pain of his loss set in and produced a painting of the cloud where he believed he saw his mother's face. It is now kept by Molly at her home. Lawrence was lost in his own grief, not knowing how to carry on without Lily. He took a lot of photographs of Lily with his newly-acquired Polaroid camera as she lay in a coma for ten days, close-ups of her clasped hands, for example, which he painted later several times, paintings that have been kept by Molly Isherwood.

Lily's coffin was laid on Lawrence's blue and white Lincoln College scarf in the front room at 'Leywood' (151 Wigan Lane) before she was laid to rest with Harry in Gidlow Cemetery. Whilst she was lying in her coffin Isherwood took more Polaroid photographs of her.

He painted his mother many times. His favourite picture of her was 'Lancashire Madonna', a large oil painting which depicted her standing in front of a cross wearing a headscarf and looking down at her clasped hands. In the bottom right-hand corner Isherwood painted in Blackie, the family cat, which died two weeks after his mother.

He was never tempted to part with this painting, even when he received generous offers for it. I was present in the art gallery of the Chapman Building at the University of Salford when he was asked about the meaning of this painting by Helen Wickham, wife of the then Bishop of Middleton. Isherwood explained that it depicted all the suffering that Lancashire women had endured in the Lancashire mills, "crucified by the cotton industry". The painting was almost completely destroyed in a fire at 151 Wigan Lane in 1983. Its burnt remains have been kept by Molly Isherwood.

If Mother Lily liked one of her son's paintings he would put a ringed 'L' on the back of it. He often painted multiple copies of a painting and the 'L' would go on the back of the one Mother Lily liked the most. What they both saw as his best paintings were kept in bank vaults.

Lawrence always put the estimated sale price of his paintings on the back of them in guineas (21s or £1.05p) along with his title for the painting, but these were very ambitious estimates and most of his paintings sold for far less than half those prices. There is usually a cross on the back of an Isherwood, which is a symbol for 'God help me'. When he first started exhibiting in Malta the price in guineas changed to the price in pounds.

A friend from Southport invited him to go back to her home on the day of Lily's funeral. In the evening they went out for a drink and called into Hagarty's shop in Eastbank Street, where he often sold his paintings. They had commissioned a painting from him of Rochdale Town Hall and had the canvas and a series of photographs in the shop ready for him. On the day after his mother's funeral he returned to the shop to execute the painting. In his own words: "I just plonked it [the paint] on automatically, and it was one of the best pictures I have ever done".

Lawrence always told people that he painted when he felt the 'bite', whether the 'bite' was caused by poverty, grief or depression. The loss of his mother was an important watershed in his life. He knew that Mother Lily wanted him to continue to display his talents in her absence.

Isherwood often fell out with people; he was very difficult to get close to. After a bout of anger he could paint even better. Bill Amos, editor of *Lancashire Life,* called him the 'Stormy Petrel'.

He was an admirer of the works of Vincent Van Gogh and especially of Toulouse Lautrec. I think he would have preferred to live their lifestyle and in their era. Isherwood also admired the work of other artists such as Miro, Manet, Picasso and Lowry, and occasionally emulated their style.

NADIA WEINER AND THE EARLY 1970S

After Mother Lily passed away, Isherwood travelled alone. It was on a visit to Oxford University in 1971 that he met a young student, Nadia Weiner, who became one of his closest friends. On one occasion he gave Nadia a lift home to Retford in Nottinghamshire, where he met her parents. Jean and Nadia Weiner visited Wigan several times and bought a collection of Isherwoods. They left to live in Australia in 1975, but Nadia returned several times to England and always made a point of contacting Lawrence. I met her on more than one occasion. After his mother died Nadia was the first to encourage him to keep painting. Isherwood was back in Oxford, at Brasenose College, in October 1972.

Isherwood's '148th one-man show in 22 years' was held on 24 March 1971 at the home of Mr Tom and Mrs Marjorie Stokes, Deane House, 123 Wigan Road Bolton, where he exhibited 60 original oils. Those in one room were on loan and not for sale and those in another room were for sale, with 10% of the takings going to the charities supported by St Mary's Church, Deane.

In 1972, Isherwood displayed 42 paintings at the Scarisbrick Hotel in Southport from 6-15 January and held his one hundred and fiftieth one-man show there from 15-29 April, "by kind permission of Mr Carey, Manager", when he exhibited 50 paintings, including 'Mother Lily in Gold Hat', 'Portrait of Lady Hayter', 'Sir Francis Chichester on Board Gypsy Moth', on sale for 35 guineas, and 'Portrait of L S Lowry at 80', on sale for 33 guineas.

An article in the *Oxford Mail* on 21 November 1972 reported that Isherwood, then aged 55, had refused to go ahead with another show at the Oxford Students' Arts Centre in Worcester Place due to the insecurity of the building. Instead, at the suggestion of the Manager of the Tackley Hotel in High Street where he was staying, Isherwood put on a show in his bedroom.

BILLINGE HOSPITAL

After Mother Lily died Lawrence started to drink more. By 1974 he was consuming two bottles of spirits a day and heading towards alcohol poisoning. His physical condition deteriorated badly and there were periods when he was unable to paint. Geoffrey Shryhane[4] transported him to Billinge Hospital where, in a near suicidal condition and unable to walk, he was admitted to C1 Psychiatric Ward on 2 August 1974. There Dr Harry Fleming, the Consultant Psychiatrist, treated him with sympathy; he went on to become a life-long friend. After about eight months in the hospital Isherwood was ready to be discharged. He entered weighing 16 stone and left weighing 14 stone.

As a Labour councillor in Bolton during our friendship I found he wasn't really interested in politics, but I always detected in him a right-wing streak. If famous people, politicians or otherwise, annoyed him he would paint grotesque pictures of them.

In 1974 he portrayed Mary Whitehouse in the nude with five breasts and titled the oil painting 'Sanctity'. The painting was purchased for £5 by the then Director of the BBC, Sir Hugh Carleton Green, whose organisation had to suffer the criticism of the Viewers' and Listeners' Association which Mrs Whitehouse fronted. The London *Evening Standard* obituary on Isherwood, published on 20 June 1989, reported that Sarah, the widow of Hugh Green, still had this painting.

In 1973 Isherwood produced a controversial oil painting depicting Captain Mark Philips kissing a half nude Princess Anne, entitled 'The First Kiss'. He hung it in the French Bar at the Scarisbrick Hotel, where it was on display for only 90 minutes, according to an article that appeared in the *Southport Visiter* on 13 September 1973. It was bought for £75 by Trevor Williamson of Gosport in Hampshire, who operated a hovercraft service from Southport beach at that time.

Dusty Springfield (1966; a picture of her in the nude sold to Hampshire pig farmer Victor Rawlings for 75 guineas), Sandy Shaw, Cilla Black, Lulu, Elizabeth Taylor, Marianne Faithful, Tommy Steele (who he painted with two heads; this painting was advertised for sale on the internet for £6,000 in 2012), Jacqueline Kennedy, Mandy Rice Davies, George Best ('Georgina Breast'; Best with breasts), the model Twiggy, Harold Wilson and Barbara Castle (1967; her nude body adorned with traffic signs - inspired by his infuriation with traffic wardens) all attracted Isherwood's attention for ridicule. When Dusty Springfield's agent complained about her portrait, Isherwood covered her up with a duster.

He exploited too the publicity surrounding the publication of *Lady Chatterley's Lover* by D H Lawrence. His 'Lady Chatterley's Lover' paintings were first put on display at the Coffee House in London between 12 June and 8 July 1961 at what he claimed was his '50th One-Man Show'. Later he depicted Mrs Thatcher as 'Miss Piggy'. In 1964 he painted the Beatles with bald heads ('The Bald Beats Maybe AD 2024') and John Lennon and the Rolling Stones crucified. Altogether 33 'personalities' received similar treatment. These controversial paintings gave Isherwood the publicity he was seeking.

Whilst in Billinge Hospital Isherwood organised art classes for other patients, which the staff of the psychiatry wards welcomed because they provided therapy for their patients. However, these were not incident free. On one occasion a nurse invaded the room that had been set aside for these classes and decided to clear it up, deciding what should stay and what should be thrown out. Isherwood grabbed hold of her and ushered her out of the room. Her complaint to the management that Isherwood had attacked her resulted in him having to apologise to the nurse for the sake of peace, but he always felt that he was the aggrieved party in this dispute.

On more than one occasion Isherwood left the hospital for a non-alcoholic drink in a local pub. Molly and Gordon Isherwood occasionally accompanied him on these trips. On one of these excursions a patient called Al persuaded Isherwood to accompany him to the Unicorn public house nearby. Whilst Isherwood stuck to ginger beer, unfortunately Al returned to the hospital much the worse for the alcohol he had consumed. Al was being treated for alcoholism, so the hospital staff were not amused by this incident.

During the time Isherwood was in hospital he commissioned Geoffrey Shryhane and Alan Bell, an estate agent in Wigan, to organise art shows for him and sell his paintings.

1974: *I AM ISHERWOOD*

Isherwood's star was on the rise in 1974. He was 57 years old and recognition was long overdue. On Tuesday 30 April 1974 the BBC broadcast *I am Isherwood*, a 30-minute documentary on his life and paintings, produced by Douglas Boyd. Douglas Boyd described Isherwood as: "...a man living in the wrong age, living in the Paris 1900 style but in Wigan in the 1970s."

Appropriately, the documentary opened with Isherwood at Wigan Pier, which he painted several times. He was then shown at various other venues in Wigan – the Parish Church, the Market Hall, the Plantations "at the back of Wigan Lane", and walking along the Leeds and Liverpool canal. "In the autumn I like to get out in Wigan, to see me through the dark days of winter", reported Isherwood.

He was filmed painting a 'Lancashire Nude' at the Scarisbrick Hotel. "I like doing nudes......To me a body speaks like a face.... Colour is what I am always seeking", commented Isherwood.

"Nature's at its best in September and October", Isherwood told his audience as he stood on Rivington Pike looking at Lord Leverhulme's dovecote on the crest of the pike.

He called it a folly. Then he commented on his love of Prussian blue: "Earth looks blue from space", he said. "I think I paint in patterns. That's what the French Impressionists did".,

Commenting on a race meeting at Haydock Park he said: "There is a marvellous atmosphere here; it's another world....It's a great challenge to put the scene down on canvas." At a show in the Bottle and Glass public house in Rainford he told his television audience: "I do it myself [selling his paintings], I don't trust agents."

Talking about the death of his mother he said: "I want to do a painting of her hands, but I can't get down to it."

In Gidlow Cemetery at the graveside of his mother and father Isherwood said: "I just feel like staying here and lying down with her....Without Mother Lily I am absolutely lost....I feel like a puppet in a way. She is guiding me to do this work."

The documentary ended at 151 Wigan Lane with Isherwood painting to music belting out of a radio set. "You do better work if you are lonely.... This is the job, I'm a painter.... I think my paintings are getting better as I get older....It's a most satisfying job....If I couldn't do it I would die....My problem is that I live and work in Wigan 1974."

Douglas Boyd set out to do a short piece on Isherwood but ended up producing a masterpiece, thirty minutes long. That TV documentary brought his paintings to the attention of a much wider audience. A very complimentary editorial in the *Wigan Observer* reported that:

> "The death of his inspiring mother left a void in Isherwood's life. But James Lawrence Isherwood was his own inspiration on Tuesday night and his brush should now move with a new purpose."

SALFORD ART GALLERY

An exhibition of his work at Salford Art Gallery, which coincided with the television documentary in 1974, was a sell-out - every painting on display found a buyer. People queued to buy his oils. Mary Robinson was one of those at Salford Art Gallery who helped to put on this watershed exhibition. She told me that, sadly, Isherwood was too drunk to attend the opening of his own exhibition.

After visiting the Salford exhibition Stephen Dixon, Art Critic for *The Guardian* newspaper, wrote in the *Arts Guardian* on 2 May 1974:

> "Lawrence Isherwood, a great and uncompromising artist in the Impressionist style, a man of awesome talent and much-vaunted poverty, exhibits 'Emotion in Paint' at Salford Art Gallery until May 18. But 'Mother Lily', who dominated his work and his affection, died at the age of 79 three years ago, and Mr Isherwood is the first to admit that the loss of her catalystic influence has been traumatic and affected his painting badly.
>
> All the same, an emotionally-handicapped Isherwood can still knock most of the others into a cocked hat and there are many good things on offer. I predict that he will be collected when most of today's artists are forgotten. It is to be hoped that this fine and honourable painter will come to terms with his grief before too long: there is still much good work to be done."

In the autumn of 1974 Margaret Purchase, a student at Chorley Adult College of Education, whose home was in Blackburn, decided to make Isherwood the subject of a dissertation that she was required to write as part of her course. She tape-recorded two interviews with him at Billinge Hospital in the early part of 1975. I met her once or twice and was pleased that she had chosen Lawrence as the subject of her study.

SUCCESS IN WIGAN

Smallman Agencies hung 180 of Isherwood's paintings in their premises at 57 Library Street, Wigan and sold the lot between 23 and 26 August 1974 (a Bank Holiday weekend). Initially there was room to hang only 80 Isherwoods, but, as they were sold, his agents replaced them with more. Some of them he had painted twenty years before the exhibition; others he had painted in Billinge Hospital and they were collected and hung wet. This exhibition was reviewed by Granada TV's *What's on in the North* bulletin on the Thursday before it opened.

It was at this exhibition that an original oil painting of Mosley Common colliery was exhibited along with some of his other best works, such as 'The Sad Eyed Clown'. Visitors pleaded with his agents to sell both of these paintings, and it was the demand for them that led Geoffrey Shryhane and Alan Bell to decide to make limited editions of prints of both of them. In the end only the Mosley Common colliery oil painting was turned into prints - a limited edition of 850. It was titled 'The Lancashire Mine'.

Previously, in 1971 and 1972, Henry Donn, who had a gallery at Whitefield and produced prints of some of L S Lowry's paintings, produced limited editions of 75 prints of Isherwood's oil paintings entitled 'Gracie Fields',

'Montgomery of Alamein' (1970), and another of Francis Chichester and Gypsy Moth (1972). Entitled 'The Lone Adventurer', signed copy number 17 of this limited edition was on sale on the internet for £240 in 2012. Some of these prints were countersigned by the personalities Isherwood painted. Henry Donn was Isherwood's agent for a short period beginning in 1971. In a publicity leaflet Isherwood used between 1955 and 1966 he named Rodney Bennett-England of 17 Adam's Row in Mayfair as his 'London agent'.

Various newspapers brought his eccentric behaviour to the attention of the general public. Before meeting him I remembered seeing him more than once on television dressed in a long grey free-flowing clerical cloak and wearing sandals without socks. With his shoulder-length hair, characteristic beard and moustache, and black heavy-rimmed glasses he looked quite mad. He certainly stood out in the Wigan landscape and the locals mocked his lifestyle.

When the Wigan exhibition was planned, Isherwood only agreed on condition that he would not have to leave Billinge Hospital to attend because he could not stand further rejection from Wiganers. On the Saturday night he attended the exhibition, but only after the visitors had all gone. He was overwhelmed by what he saw and heard.

Isherwood was especially disappointed that Wigan Borough Council had shown no interest in the paintings on display at this exhibition. He thought they might be particularly interested in a large pencil drawing of the 'Squirrel Inn in Scholes' or of an oil painting of the 'Royal George Common Lodging House', which was bought for £60 by a Mrs Mary Maye, who lived in a council flat built on the site.

Isherwood is reported to have said: "The old Wigan

Corporation never took me seriously. I thought they would have bought this time, but no. I doubt if I will sell them anything in future. Now, I have little confidence in them. It works both ways, you know."

In a letter dated 26 November 1974, addressed to Margaret Purchase, the Arts Officer at Wigan Museum (now Wigan Arts and Heritage Services), Neil Hanson, identified six Isherwood paintings that were in their collection at that time: 'Lowry at 84', 'Wigan Top Lock', 'Self Portrait', 'Queen Street, Wigan', 'Pit Lassies', 'Victoria Colliery', and 'Wigan Arms', all oils purchased in 1973. These paintings can be seen at www.bbc.co.uk/arts/yourpaintings (although the titles are slightly different, for example 'Portrait of a Man' is probably the same painting as 'Self Portrait') which displays a 'gallery' of 14 of Isherwood's paintings.

After the Wigan show another was organised by Smallman Agencies at the Town Hall in Chorley, with 40 original oil paintings on display. It opened on Saturday 26 October and 'The Miner' was the painting of greatest interest to the 2,000 visitors, on sale at £70. It was the first painting to be sold. The Chorley show was followed by one at the Brocket Arms in Mesnes Road, Wigan from 12-13 December 1974, also organised by Smallman Agencies.

ISHERWOOD SACKS HIS WIGAN AGENTS

In March 1975 Isherwood sacked his agents Geoffrey Shryhane and Alan Bell after they had produced the limited edition of prints entitled 'The Lancashire Mine' (reproduced from an oil painting of Mosley Common colliery), which he had sketched one night in 1961 from a lay-by on the East

Lancashire Road (the A580) en route to an engagement at Granada TV Studios in Manchester. In characteristic style he told the *Wigan Evening Post* that he had sacked his agents without telling them first. "To sack the people he had appointed his agents by going to the newspapers was indeed the dirtiest of tricks and one that was totally unforgivable", Geoffrey Shyhane told me.

Isherwood claimed that they had demanded a 60% commission on the sale of his paintings, which annoyed him. Before Shryhane and Bell had laid out a large sum of money to have 'The Lancashire Mine' turned into prints, Isherwood told Shryhane, "You pay for it to be printed and give me a £1 a signature. Lowry gets £4."

Soon after the prints were published, Isherwood demanded a 50% commission on the sales without offering to make a contribution towards the printing costs; he signed about 350 of these prints. The rest were stored under my bed at Woburn Avenue in Bolton for several months.

Isherwood dragged Dr Harry Fleming, his Consultant Psychiatrist at Billinge Hospital, into the row with his agents. In an interview with Susan (Sue) Darling, reported in the *Wigan Post and Chronicle* of 12 March 1975, Dr Fleming said:

> "He came in here [Billinge Hospital] with debts, and I was wondering how a man of so many years' work was failing to pay his debts. I found out he had agents who were taking 60% of his profits for picture sales. I thought this was a bit much in view of the fact that he is getting on in life, he was in this financial situation, and in a depressed state in hospital."

Dr Fleming went on to tell Sue that he had approached Alan Bell in an abortive bid to get him to forego some of the commission: “I put my feelings to him quite directly, but he told me he was a business man and could not listen. Jim Isherwood should be better off from now on, because he has good friends to advise him on running his own affairs.”

Dr Fleming knew that Frank and Marjorie Carey and I were trying to help Lawrence. Geoffrey Shryhane and Alan Bell defended their position and denied that their ‘commission’ was as high as was claimed by Isherwood, but they refused to reveal what it was. They claimed that the commission had been agreed by Isherwood before they undertook to be his agents. They said: “The figure of 60% is rubbish. Our commission may have been higher on the exhibitions because we had to frame and varnish many paintings, which is a job not usually undertaken by agents.”

Isherwood also complained to me later that no record was kept of the sales by his ‘agents’ at these exhibitions or of how much they had sold the paintings for or who they had sold them to.

Geoffrey Shryhane told me that, during one of his visits to see Isherwood in Billinge Hospital to discuss their first exhibition and any commission arising from it, he had said: “It’s 50:50. I can’t sell any [of his paintings], so why should you?” Shryhane believes that, as Isherwood saw how much demand there was for his paintings when they were properly marketed, he regretted making this informal agreement.

Geoffrey Shryhane and Alan Bell arranged a launch of ‘The Lancashire Mine’ prints at the Grand Hotel in Wigan in February 1975, and invited the miners’ leader Joe Gormley to receive the first signed print. Wigan’s MP Alan Fitch was also present. At first Isherwood refused to attend but, after 'prolonged and difficult negotiations', he agreed to be there. Joe Gormley co-signed 10 of these prints. Geoffrey Shryhane did not speak to Isherwood again after their 'fall-out', although he continued to recognise his talent and collect his paintings.

Over the years Isherwood tried to contact Shryhane at his office by telephone but Shryhane refused to have anything to do with him. "It was a matter of principle. The artist had treated others in the same irrational manner. He was at war with himself", Shryhane told me.

I MEET ISHERWOOD IN SOUTHPORT

Isherwood's 'fall-out' with Geoffrey Shryhane and Alan Bell coincided with an exhibition of 105 Isherwood paintings (13 watercolours; the rest were oil paintings), which Frank and Marjorie Carey promoted at the Scarisbrick Hotel in Southport, where Merrilyn and I met him on 15 March 1975 in the Derby Room (see the prologue to this book). The exhibition, which was opened by His Honour Judge Pigot QC on 12 March, was open to the public from 13-16 March 1975. Bernard Clarke interviewed Lawrence at the Scarisbrick Hotel on 12 March for a piece Bob Greaves presented on *Granada Reports* that evening.

Isherwood was initially given three days' 'leave' followed by another three days and then a month by Billinge Hospital to organise and attend this exhibition. The Careys provided a room at the hotel (room 202) where he could live, recuperate and paint. Effectively they became his patrons. He had a horror of returning to live at 151 Wigan Lane without Mother Lily. Frank and Marjorie Carey took him abroad for the first time, to Spain – Malaga and Torremolinos - which attracted

Isherwood to make several trips to the sun in the following years, including a visit to Majorca with Gordon and Molly Isherwood. Billinge Hospital discharged Isherwood whilst he was staying at the Scarisbrick Hotel, in March 1975.

Isherwood billed himself as 'England's Foremost Impressionist Painter', a title given to him by the media. I have watched him paint several times, both at 151 Wigan Lane and during exhibitions I organised for him. Usually his first application of oil paint on a white board would be a covering of his favourite Prussian blue colour. Other oil colours were squeezed out of tubes onto a board, which acted as his palette, and applied thickly on top of the Prussian blue. He manipulated the oils with various brushes as well as with the tips of the brushes, his palette knife and his fingers. Isherwood could paint with amazing speed when he felt 'the bite'. He used the primary colours, red, green and blue, to great effect.

Isherwood often painted from photographs he had taken of people or scenes, sometimes directly from the television screen, with his Polaroid camera or from pictures he liked in magazines. He rarely painted outdoors, preferring instead to make a rough sketch on any bit of paper that he had available, or even on the back of his hand, if his Polaroid camera was not to hand.

'LEYWOOD', 151 WIGAN ROAD

I first visited 151 Wigan Lane with him while he was staying at the Scarisbrick Hotel recovering from his stay in hospital. He made great play of the fact that he was drinking ginger beer or blackcurrant juice at that time. As Lawrence unlocked the door of his home we couldn't get in at first. The reason was that piles of mail lay behind it. Eventually we pushed the door open far enough to be able to throw the piles of papers to the back of the hall. As we finally entered it was a scene of utter chaos.

The hallway was littered with unopened mail and other paperwork; Lawrence hadn't picked it up to open for years, never mind months. We immediately entered the 'back room' where he painted. The table was strewn with empty bottles, boards, half-finished paintings, palettes and brushes and bric-a-brac of every kind. There was hardly room to put a foot down. The room reeked of turpentine and oil paint.

The house was heated only by a coal fire, at either side of which were Isherwood's and Mother Lily's chairs. A small oil painting of Blackie the cat, which I always admired, stood on the mantelpiece and I caught sight of an easily recognisable portrait of Gandhi amongst the rubbish on the table.

I spent many hours in that room talking to Lawrence, often into the early hours of the morning. He didn't start painting until well gone midnight and was rarely up before midday. A barely readable notice on the front door read 'No callers before 3.30 pm', after which time he (and previously his mother) 'came round'.

The front downstairs room was a similar scene of chaos. A double bed occupied much of the room but that was strewn with Isherwood's paintings, some finished, some not. There were paintings under the bed and piled around the bed in unorganised heaps. Many of these paintings were sold by the Isherwood family later. Lawrence had either used them in exhibitions or abandoned them for one reason or another. It wasn't difficult to find a painting amongst these heaps that a visitor liked enough to purchase from him. I took two of my visitors from Bolton's twin town Paderborn there on separate occasions, and each bought paintings from this collection.

Likewise, the rest of the house, including Lawrence's bedroom, was part of the general chaos of living with Isherwood. The gardens around the house were a jungle.

AINTREE

After Mrs Topham, the owner of Aintree race course, died, there was a period when Grand National weekends were abandoned. Then Bill Davies, a Merseyside contractor, whose multi-million-pound company the Walton Group purchased the race course and re-opened it in 1975, contacted Lawrence and commissioned a mural of 'Becher's Brook' from him, which they intended to display in the reception room at Aintree. They offered the miserable fee of £200, which barely covered the cost of the materials. I purchased all the materials Lawrence needed to execute this painting. Lawrence's paintings of race courses and horses show the excitement and emotion of the events. His paintings give the impression that the horses and their jockeys are actually moving on the canvas.

Isherwood painted one of his best racecourse scenes ever, and the mural was mounted in time for the Grand National weekend at Aintree. A row broke out between Bill Davies and Isherwood, who believed that he was not going to be paid for executing the mural. This row was reported by the *Southport Visiter* on 8 and 15 March 1975. Isherwood said of the fee offered by Bill Davies for the commission:

> "It's bloody ridiculous. I suggested that they should get a painter and decorator to do it for that price – if he would. To me, £1,000 would be a more realistic offer......Now I have decided to kick the thing into

> touch and do a skit on Bill Davies with horns as one of the Four Horsemen of the Apocalypse in an Aintree setting. I started it today and it should be finished by Tuesday, ready for the exhibition, where it will sell for £350." (This painting is in the Isherwood family collection today.)

Hours before the exhibition at the Scarisbrick Hotel was due to open, on 12 March 1975, Bill Davies settled his row with Isherwood. The mural is now in the ownership of the White family (see later).

Before the row was settled, Lawrence approached me with the preposterous suggestion that we break into Aintree race course and steal the painting back. He was going to tip Granada TV off about this event! Of course, I rejected his offer.

Isherwood received three tickets for the 1975 Grand National and he invited me and Merrilyn to accompany him to the event on the Saturday, but we declined. He attended. He was a prolific letter writer and we kept all his letters. The first was written to us on 2 April 1975. It contained a mention of these invitations and reported to us that he was "jiggered" - a word used a lot by Lawrence – "after the G/Nat [Grand National] LOT" and was going to the cinema.

ISHERWOOD'S 'REBIRTH' IN SALFORD

When I met Isherwood I was teaching chemistry and running a research group at the University of Salford. The Chapman Building, a newly completed building on the university's campus, was a suite of lecture theatres, but it housed some workshops and a coffee bar as well as a small art gallery. I suggested to Isherwood that I try to organise a show for him there. After all, Salford Art Gallery, on the same campus as the university at that time, was where he had enjoyed his most successful exhibition ever. He had almost died after an exhibition in Salford. It seemed sensible to bring him back to Salford to be 'reborn'.

From the moment that I suggested another show in Salford and right up to the opening moment, I had many meetings with Isherwood, usually at the Scarisbrick Hotel in Southport, trying to convince him that I would do everything possible to make the show a success. It was very difficult at first to get close to him and make him believe that I was not just another hanger-on. We sat talking until the early hours of the morning and I often drove down Lord Street on my way home to Bolton as dawn broke, with seagulls sweeping ahead of me down the roadway. In the end I think that I convinced him that, like Frank Carey, I was seriously interested in his work and his future in painting and not in exploiting him.

The show at the University of Salford, 'Sober Emotion in Paint', was opened on 22 April 1975 by Douglas J Edwards, High Sheriff of the County of Greater Manchester, and the response from the public was amazing. Lawrence was there throughout the exhibition, which closed on 2 May. He sold paintings so fast that we ended up selling the ones he had just finished, the oils still not dry. Molly and Gordon Isherwood took over £1,000 for him in under two hours during the preview. Several of my colleagues at the university attended and purchased Isherwoods. Professor Hans Suschitzky and his wife Judith bought a Southport beach landscape. Frank and Marjorie Carey were there too.

We listed 108 paintings altogether in the catalogue but we probably sold at least another 50, mainly oils. After this experience it was clear that there was a huge demand for Isherwood's paintings. On pages 27-28 of *Isherwood* by Stephen Eckersley there is confusion between the 1974 exhibition at Salford Art Gallery and the 1975 show I organised at the University of Salford.

On the afternoon of 22 April BBC TV visited and gave the exhibition some publicity that evening on their programme *Look North*. Andrew Grimes, the Political Correspondent of the *Manchester Evening News* and also a friend of mine, wrote a major piece on Isherwood in their paper, which appeared on Thursday 24 April 1975.

Shortly after we met Isherwood he told us about Ellen Bate, who was well-known in Bolton as a poet, artist and

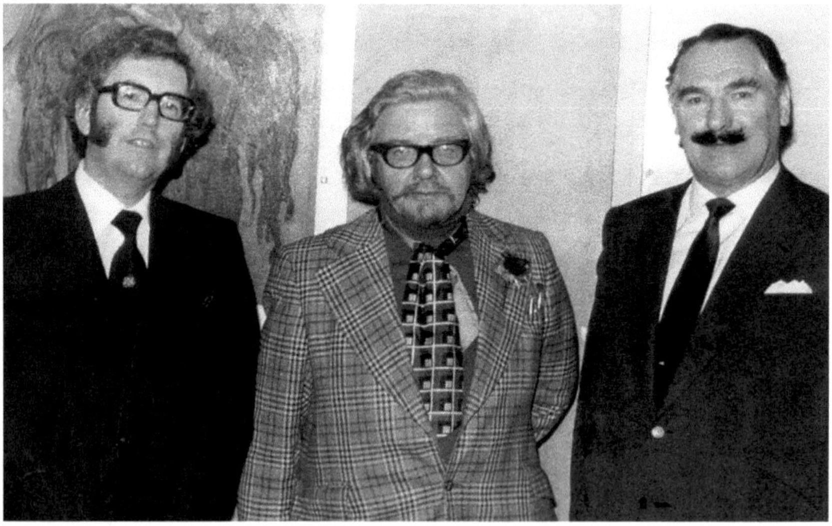

Left to right: Frank Carey, James Lawrence Isherwood and Douglas J Edwards (former Lord Mayor of Manchester) at the opening of the show at the University of Salford in 1975.

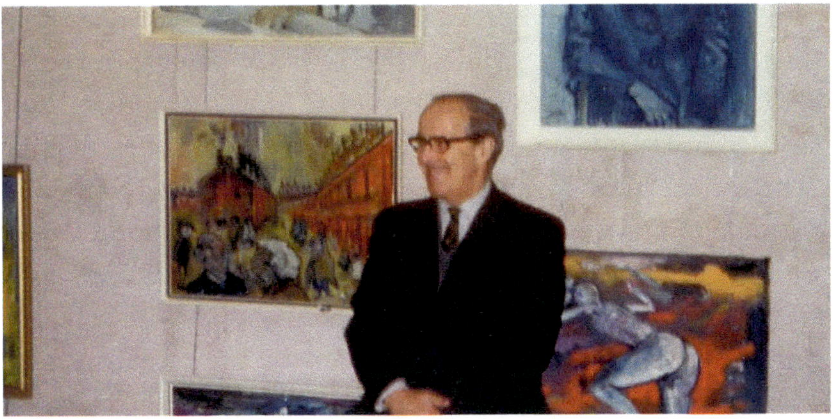

Professor Hans Suschitzky at the University of Salford show in 1975.

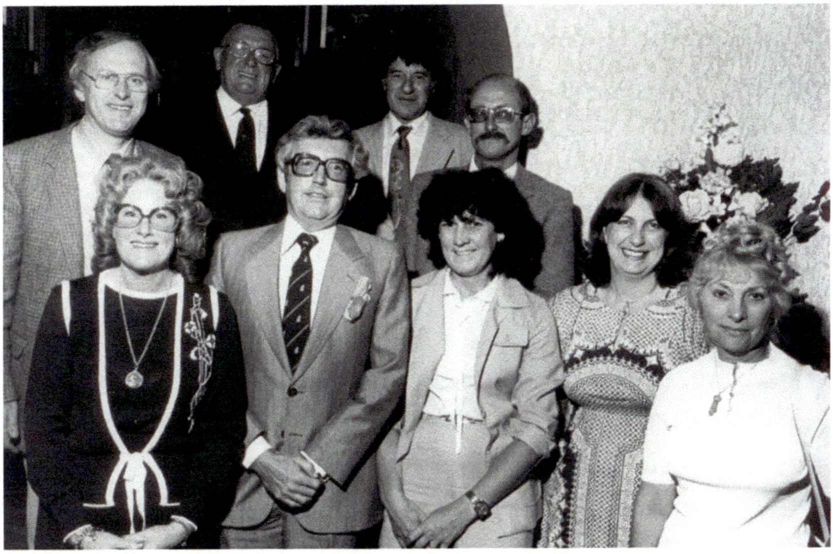

One of the weekend gatherings at the Scarisbrick Hotel.

Back row: Dr. Brian Iddon, Bertie Dawson, Lou Fine (a record producer who worked with Hughie Green) and Tony Hale (Head of Music at Capitol Radio).

Front row: Marjorie and Frank Carey, Mrs. Hale, Merrilyn Iddon and Mrs. Fine. (Picture by Graham Sherrif, Photographics, Southport).

artist's model. He had persuaded Ellen to pose for one of his series of 'Lancashire Nudes' over twenty years previously. When we told him that Ellen had died from a drugs overdose in December 1974 at the age of 50, Lawrence decided to paint 'The Dead Nude' for the show at the University of Salford as a tribute to her life. Initially, according to a report in the *Bolton Evening News* (26 March 1975), Ellen's mother Alice Bate, who was in her 70s at the time and lived in Queensgate, Bolton, said she had no objections to the proposal but, after being shown photographs of the painting, she became critical of it (according to a report in the *Bolton Evening News* on 18 April 1975). I was uneasy about Isherwood generating publicity for the exhibition at the University of Salford using this painting. But, if you worked with Isherwood, you had to take him warts and all.

I spent a lot of time in the Chapman Building Art Gallery when Lawrence had his show at the university, as did my first wife Merrilyn; both Lawrence and I talked to a lot of people and we tape-recorded a lot of their conversations. I still have the four tape cassettes from those days.

Several people who visited Isherwood's exhibitions said "I do a bit of painting myself". After a while, whenever we heard this expression or a person say "I paint myself", we had difficulty in not laughing. Lawrence told me that he envisaged these people with their clothes off painting themselves. It became a joke that only Lawrence and my family understood.

During 1975 Lawrence regularly visited us at Woburn Avenue in Bolton and often stayed overnight. While the exhibition was running at the University of Salford he stayed in our home, although I returned him to the Scarisbrick Hotel in Southport one weekend, where he painted more oils for his exhibition. We visited several of the local restaurants and public houses during the two weeks of the exhibition, including The Lamb on the Bradshaw-Hawkshaw Road and The Pack Horse at Affetside. 1 May 1975 was the day of the local elections, and we finished up in Tonge Ward Labour Club.

A Mrs Lowry[5] visited the exhibition at the University of Salford; her husband was a relative of L S Lowry, and her daughter had been encouraged by him to become an art teacher. Mrs Lowry was present when Roy Cross came to interview Lawrence for Radio Manchester. "Being sober, I'm more vicious", Lawrence told Roy. "I'm more versatile than Lowry", he added in an attempt to provoke Mrs Lowry to join in the interview. But she was having none of it.

Talking about the people in his Wigan landscapes Isherwood told a man from Blackpool: "I make them look like lost creatures in a lost world. When I do horses I'm interested in making them move. It's the same with netball players or rugby players."

In 1975 Lawrence painted two portraits of my first wife Merrilyn – 'Lady in Black' and 'Lady in Mink' - both painted on canvases that I bought for Lawrence. The first portrait was of Merrilyn dressed in the black coat and hat she wore when we met Isherwood in Southport after my Uncle Dick's funeral. It was painted in two and a half hours in the art gallery at the University of Salford after the exhibition closed one day. We hung it in the gallery during the show and it was much admired by many of the visitors to Isherwood's exhibition. 'Lady in Mink', a larger and more elaborate oil painting, was painted one evening (between 5 pm and 8.40 pm, I recorded) at our home in Woburn Avenue. Merrilyn wore a fur coat for this painting but it wasn't mink!

Lawrence painted a watercolour portrait of my daughter Sheena after she presented him with a Swiss roll she had baked for him and another of the view across our back garden looking down into Firwood Fold. I remember that he liked to paint to the music from the musical 'Cabaret', which I played over and over again for him. He arrived in Bolton by train on 5 July 1975 to celebrate my birthday and presented me with a small framed picture of a female nude ('The Mirror') which he had done with pen and crayon on the train.

On 7 May 1975 he wrote a long letter to us from the Scarisbrick Hotel:

> "You've helped me to take a new great step forward – I have even more power than ever now. A new vista opens before me, new plans, fresh ambitions!! Playing it cool – but underneath I am a boiling mass. Even Laurie here [a member of staff at the Scarisbrick Hotel] and people take on a new look. I feel better – I hope it keeps up."

The rest of the letter was written with the same positivity about his future. He included two sketches in ink, one for each of my two daughters, Sally and Sheena, drawn on his pink headed notepaper. Sometimes he called them 'prawn' and 'shrimp', as on this occasion, and on other occasions he used the terms 'crab' for himself and 'shrimp' for each of the girls. Lawrence preferred to write letters to us rather than speak to us on the telephone. He often illustrated his letters with sketches, for example of crabs and shrimps.

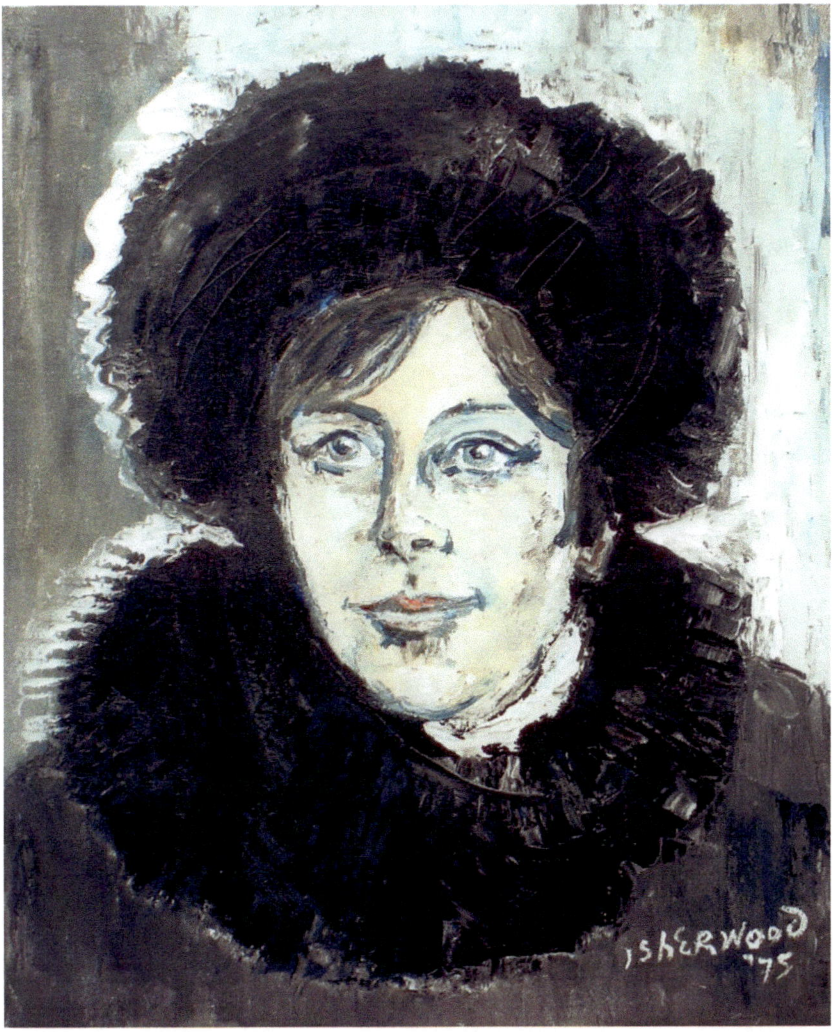

Lady in Black (1975; oil on canvas; 50 x 60 cm).

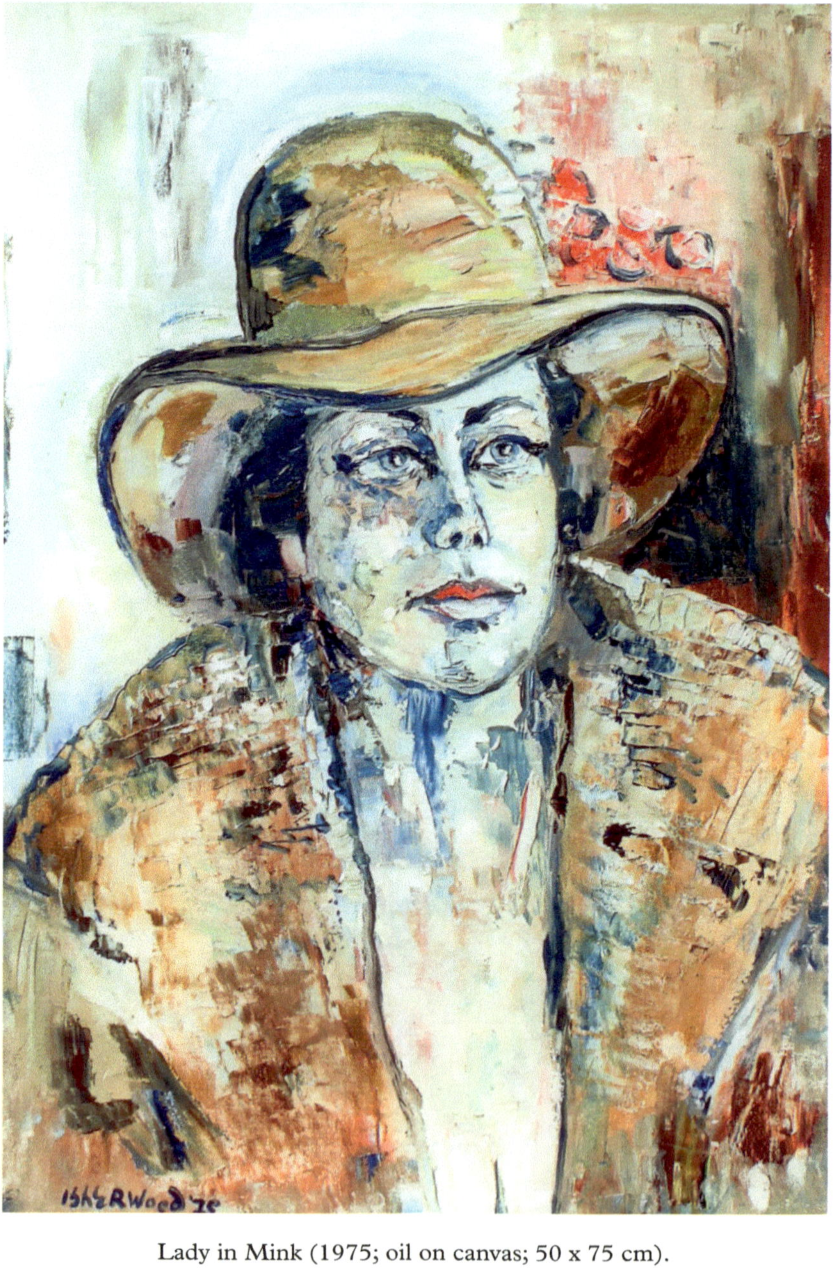

Lady in Mink (1975; oil on canvas; 50 x 75 cm).

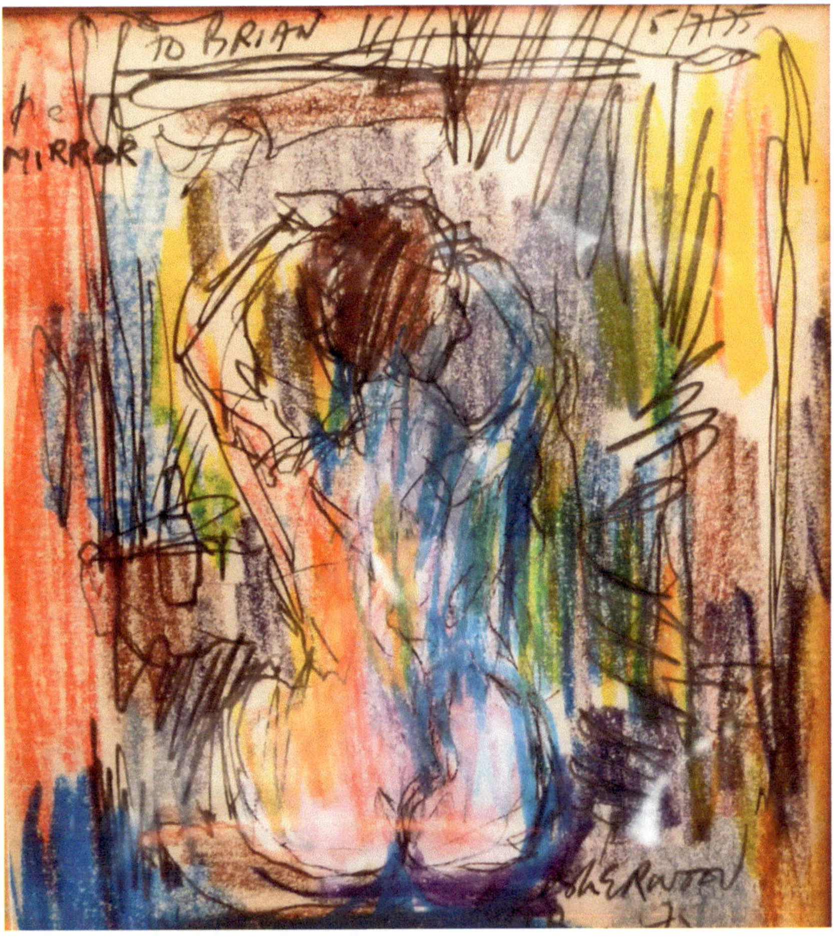

The Mirror (1975; pen and crayon on paper; 9 x 10 cm).

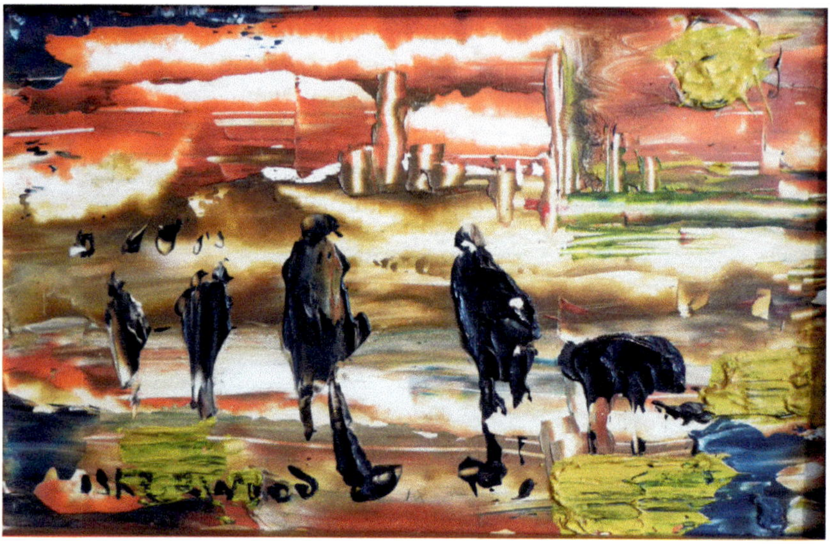

Wigan Red Sky (1975; oil on board; 9 x 15 cm).

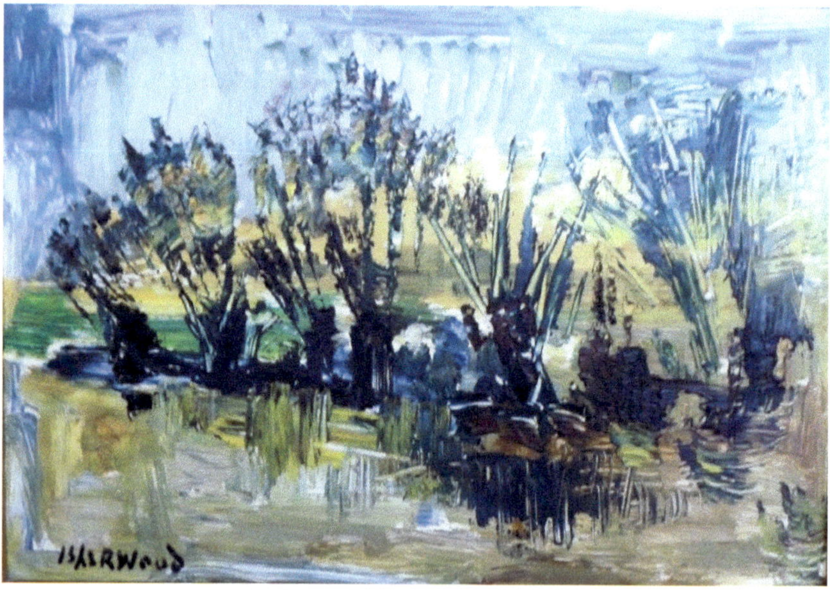

Willows, Oxford (oil on board, 25 x 25 cm).

Frank Carey and I committed ourselves to keep Lawrence painting and befriend him in such a way that he would not go through another period of his life like the one he had just experienced, before and during his admission to Billinge Hospital. Even so, Frank and Marjorie and Mark and Jill Carey (their children) and the hotel staff had some difficult and often stressful moments with Lawrence during his stay at the Scarisbrick Hotel. Frank remembers Isherwood's 'blue period', a period of about ten days when he refused to come out of room 202 or answer his telephone. Staff left his meals outside his door and collected the empty trays later.

ISHERWOOD FALLS IN LOVE WITH TRAVEL TO THE SUN

Frank and Marjorie Carey took Lawrence to Hotel Cervantes, in Torremolinos, Spain from 11-18 May 1975 along with their son Mark. "It's a new world out here" he wrote on a postcard to us dated 14 May. On 3 June 1975, the *Southport Visiter* reported him as saying, "I visited a lot of night spots in Spain to get some local colour, but I'm still on orange juice".

On his return from Spain Isherwood mounted a show, 'Isherwood in Spain', at the Scarisbrick Hotel in Southport from 5-8 June 1975. His trips to the sun with the Carey family opened his eyes to a new life and he often travelled abroad after that, sometimes on his own. His oil painting took on a new dimension.

Quite by coincidence BBC TV broadcast its 30-minute documentary *I am Isherwood* for the second time on the evening before the Southport show was due to open, on 4 June 1975, and I was able to see it and record it on an audio tape, which I have kept. The BBC failed to archive a copy of this TV documentary after it was broadcast again in 1975. I must be the only person with any record of the soundtrack of this programme.

In my opinion 1974 and 1975 were vintage years for Isherwood's artistic achievements despite his eight months' hospitalisation. After his TV appearance on 22 April, which launched his exhibition at the University of Salford, the poet Harold Morland wrote to Lawrence to say how much he had been impressed by his appearance on television and his painting style. His letter of 23 April was accompanied by a book of his poems. Morland too had suffered alcoholism and had been very close to his mother before her death. He apologised for not being able to attend Lawrence's exhibition but expressed a wish to see some of his paintings.

I suggested to Lawrence that we journey to the Lake District the following Sunday to meet Harold Morland and his sister and show them some of his paintings. The Morlands lived in a remote setting at Hill Top, Hawkshead Hill, near Ambleside. The following Sunday Lawrence and I set off in my car, with Sally, Sheena and Merrilyn, to meet the Morlands. It was a lovely sunny day and, after taking lunch at the Sun Inn in Crook, we crossed Windermere on the Ferry Nab to visit them. Although they were charming people I didn't detect much chemistry between them and Lawrence. Nevertheless, we all enjoyed our 'day out'.

During and after the show at the University of Salford Isherwood received several requests to put on other shows.

PAT WHITE APPEARS IN ISHERWOOD'S LIFE

Peter and Hazel Collinge invited Lawrence to give their well-known hairdressing business some publicity by holding a show at the Peter Collinge Salon in Market Street, Hoylake on the Wirral. 'Isherwood's Merseyside' was opened by Mrs June Lancely-Green on 25 June 1975 and ran until 2 July. I transported Lawrence and his paintings to Hoylake from the Scarisbrick Hotel and helped him to put on the show.

I remember him telephoning me the evening after the opening, very excited about an attractive woman called Pat White who had purchased an oil painting of a clown which, unusually, Lawrence had forgotten to sign. She returned the following day to get Lawrence to sign the painting, and that was the beginning of another phase in his life. She drove him to her home, Roseacre, in Neston on the Wirral in her white E-type Jaguar sports car, which impressed Lawrence greatly. Pat returned him to the Scarisbrick Hotel a few days later, on 2 July.

The University of Salford invited Laurence Stephen Lowry several times to accept an honorary degree. Finally, he accepted, and the Honorary Degree of Doctor of Letters was awarded to him at a congregation held in the Maxwell Hall at the university on Friday 11 July 1975. One of my colleagues from the Department of Chemistry and Applied Chemistry, Professor W J Orville-Thomas presented Lowry for his degree.

Lowry was so fragile that he was unable to ascend the steps to the stage, so the degree was presented to him where he sat on the front row, with others being awarded degrees on that day. "I am doing nothing at all and trying to do it as well as I can", said 87-year-old Lowry on the day.

I managed to get visitor's tickets for Lawrence and Frank Carey to attend, and Lowry and Isherwood met up at the reception held afterwards. It was a memorable day.

Isherwood's pencil sketch of the scene was reproduced in the William Hickey column in the *Daily Express* newspaper on 12 July 1975.

L S Lowry died from pneumonia in hospital on 23 February 1976.

EXAMPLES OF ISHERWOOD'S MISCHIEVOUSNESS

A regular visitor to Isherwood's exhibitions in 1975 was Father Rattigan, the priest in charge of St Hilda's Roman Catholic Church in Tottington. He was a genuine admirer of Lawrence's work and bought small Isherwoods from a number of his exhibitions. At one of them, probably his show at the University of Salford, he persuaded Lawrence to travel to his church hall to paint whilst discussing his life and work, and put on a small exhibition there on 8 August 1975. Parishioners were to be invited to admire Isherwood's technique, with an entrance fee charged to raise money for the church.

Foolishly, Lawrence accepted this commission and almost immediately rejected it. His way out was to tell the priest in late July 1975 that he would paint one of his nude paintings in the church hall and put some paintings of nudes on display too, including his nude painting of Ellen Bate. Father Rattigan was told by Lawrence that I was his manager and that he should deal with me. I denied this in the *Manchester Evening News* on 30 July 1975. However, Father Rattigan telephoned me several times and pleaded with me to get Lawrence to act reasonably. He was in quite a state at what he believed might be the end of his career as a priest. At the end of July Isherwood called the exhibition off, much to Father Rattigan's relief.

"As far as I am concerned, the whole thing is off",

Isherwood told the *Manchester Evening News*. "I have been fighting this kind of thing all my life – people who think the human body is wicked. The girl I was going to paint is very beautiful with perfect Titian hair. The priest probably wouldn't mind me showing a few old-fashioned genteel nudes. But I don't paint those. I like to show a few bottoms and tops. I am trying to educate people."

I wasn't aware of any young woman who had offered to pose for Lawrence in Tottington.

Isherwood certainly had a mischievous streak in him and would use occasions such as this to gain publicity. On one occasion, probably when I was transporting his paintings to the Hoylake show, I was loading paintings into the back of my car outside the Scarisbrick Hotel in Southport when a litter bin on a nearby lamp post burst into flames. I saw Lawrence walking away from it quickly with a smile on his face.

STEPHEN TAYLOR

Frank and Marjorie Carey were friendly with the Taylor family in Southport whose 20-year-old son Stephen was a gifted student studying sculpture at the Art College in Stafford. Merrilyn and I accompanied Lawrence and Frank and Marjorie Carey to meet the Taylors and their son in Stafford and to view some of Stephen's work at an art exhibition at his college. Afterwards we all enjoyed a dinner at the Tillington Hall Hotel, near Stafford.

Frank bought two of Stephen's life-size female nudes cast in 'cement fondue'. One stood in the Baron's Bar at the Scarisbrick Hotel for several years (it featured along with Isherwood in a picture published in the *West Lancashire Visitor* on 29 July 1975) and the other, a reclining nude, was bought to place at the side of the swimming pool at the Steak and Stilton restaurant and leisure complex at Leigh, one of three businesses owned by Frank and Marjorie Carey at that time, the third being at Burscough Bridge, near Ormskirk.

Merrilyn and I bought a much more modest-sized reclining nude from Stephen, which is still in my possession today, along with a large pencil drawing of another nude. When he left college Stephen was forced to take a job as a milkman. Today he drives a taxi in Southport.

Lawrence mounted an exhibition, 'I am Isherwood', at Bootle Art Gallery from 6-27 September 1975, his one hundred and eightieth one-man show. I was present when Bob Smithies, a Granada television presenter, opened the show on 5 September. The gallery presented 42 paintings at prices ranging from 29 to 325 guineas. There were five paintings on display that were not for sale – 'Lady in Black', 'Lady in Mink' (his portraits of my first wife Merrilyn), 'Portrait of Bob Smithies', 'Portrait of Mrs Pat White', and 'The New Clown', the painting purchased by Pat White at the Hoylake show. Isherwood fell out with Bootle Art Gallery over a dispute about the catalogue and he and Pat took the paintings down a week earlier than advertised.

Isherwood continued to paint controversial nudes of famous people. Those next in line for this treatment were the actress Vivien Merchant, MP John Stonehouse's devoted secretary Sheila Buckley and Lady Falkender (Marcia Williams before Harold Wilson created a peerage for her), whose painting, entitled 'Lady in Labour', showed her pregnant. This painting of 1976 was sold for £160 to a Tory Councillor from Brighton.

ISHERWOOD AND PAT WHITE ANNOUNCE THEIR ENGAGEMENT

Lawrence announced his engagement to Patricia White, a widow of eighteen months in her forties and with two sons, Frazer, aged 17, and Cameron, aged 20, in the *Manchester Evening News* ('Mr Manchester's Diary') on 16 September 1975 and in the *Southport Visiter* on 20 September 1975.

"I went to buy a painting [at the Hoylake show] and I got the artist", Pat said.

"It was love at first sight" said Isherwood. "I have met the perfect woman. All others had disillusioned me, but Pat is very beautiful in every way; a young Marlene Dietrich."

When her husband Kennedy died at the age of 45, Pat lived in a six-bedroom house, Roseacre, at Neston, on the Wirral, with a swimming pool in two acres of land. The Whites also owned Bryngwydd Farm, with 44 acres of land, in an isolated spot at Edern, near Nefyn, on the Lleyn Peninsula in North Wales, and a holiday flat in Spinola Bay, Malta.

TRAVEL, TRAVEL AND MORE TRAVEL

On 24 September 1975 Lawrence wrote to Frank and Marjory Carey to say that he was going with Pat to Sorrento in Italy for two weeks, to stay in the Continental Hotel. On their return he planned to visit Oxford where he and Pat would get married, with a reception at the home of Sir William and Lady Hayter in New College. He also reported that he was trying to see Gracie Fields on the Isle of Capri. Pat wrote at the bottom of the letter: "Have just read this letter – he's a liar – we're just good friends!"

Lawrence wrote to me and Merrilyn on 28 September 1975 about his engagement.

Whilst delivering some of Lawrence's paintings to the Scarisbrick Hotel in her white E-type Jaguar Pat received a fine for parking it with its two nearside tyres on the kerb. Isherwood was so incensed at this that he threatened to go to Southport Magistrate's Court on 14 October 1975 with a 10" x 20" framed oil painting on canvas, 'Southport Beach', to pay the fine (reported in *The Sunday Express* of 21 September 1975).

Mr Douglas Mason, Clerk of Southport Magistrate's Court, said: "I cannot see the lay magistrates accepting the sale of a painting for a fine – or even the picture itself as barter for the fine. But if he were to sign it on the back – like a cheque – then it might be possible. I have never heard of anything like this."

Lawrence had pulled this stunt previously. "If I can clear garage bills, hotel accounts – even my weekly rent – with my art why not a court fine?" he responded.

On 17 October 1975 we received a letter from 'Ishy' from Malta, where he and Pat were on holiday, to say that they were flying on to Naples the following day. In Malta he met Prime Minister Dom Mintoff's sister, the Marquis di Sichuna and other notables and held a one-man show in September at the Museum of Fine Arts in Valetta. On 23 October 1975 he wrote to Frank Carey from the Hotel Palatine in Rome. Pat and Lawrence also visited Mallorca before returning home to Oxford. Lawrence loved his new life in the sun.

Lawrence wrote to us on 25 November 1975 to announce their 'wedding' and he announced that he was 'married' in Mr Manchester's Diary in the *Manchester Evening News* of the same date.

Lord (Dr Michael) Winstanley, famous for his radio show *This is Your Right*, opened another Isherwood exhibition, 'Mediterranean Honeymoon', in the Derby Room at the Scarisbrick Hotel on 27 February 1976 at which Lawrence and Pat displayed 40 of their paintings of Malta and Italy. For the Southport show I returned Isherwood's prints of 'The Lancashire Mine' (Mosley Common colliery), which I had kept for a long time at my home in Bolton. At this exhibition he displayed a new portrait of L S Lowry which appeared in a piece about the exhibition in the *Lancashire Evening Post* on 2 March 1976.

I had been conscious at the exhibition of Lawrence's paintings that I put on at the University of Salford in April

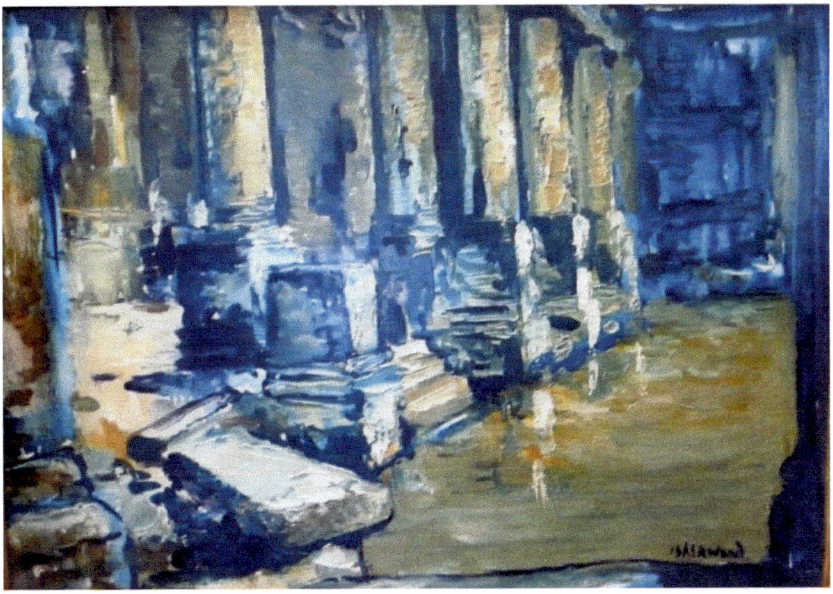

Roman Bath (1963; oil on board; 30 x 40 cm).

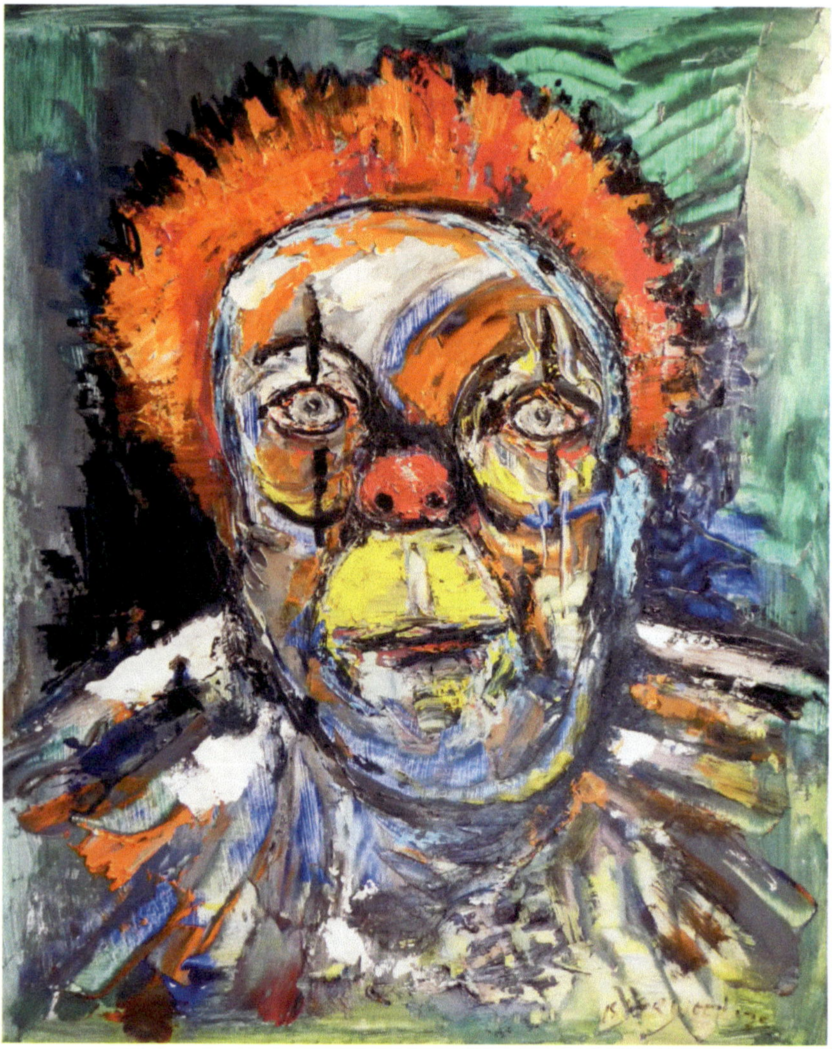

The Spanish Clown (1975; acrylic paint on canvas; 45 x 60 cm).

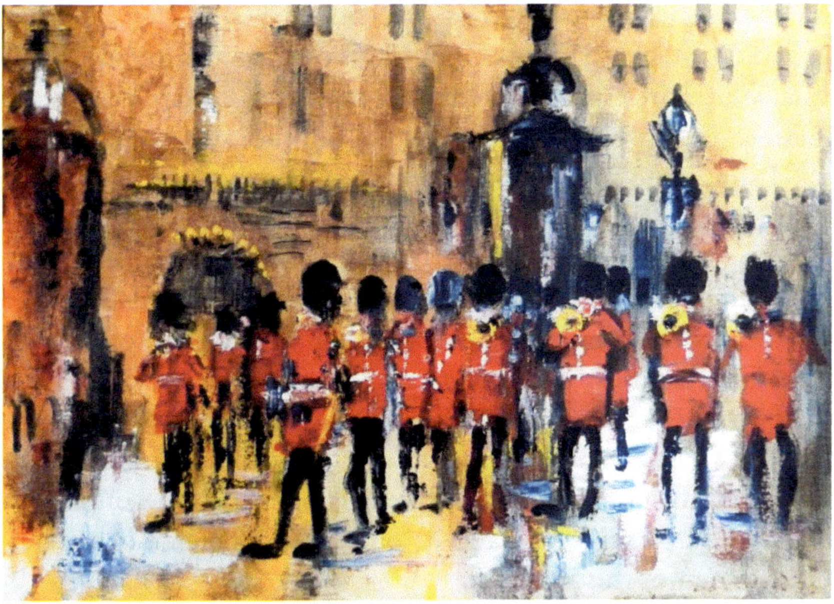

Guards at Buckingham Palace (1975; acrylic paint on canvas; 45 x 60 cm).

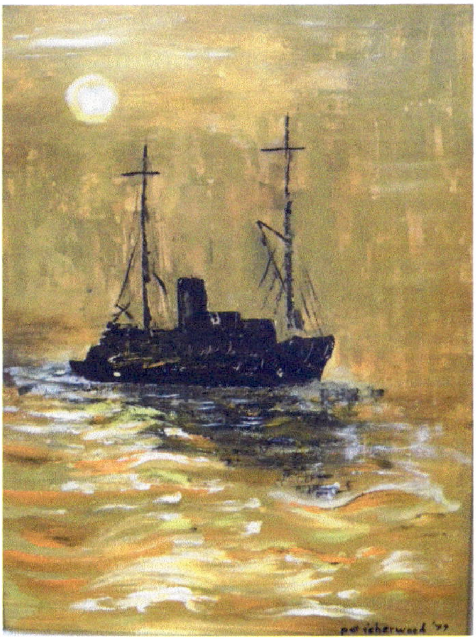

The Boat (1977; signed by Pat 'Isherwood', probably painted by Lawrence Isherwood; oil on board, 30 x 40 cm).

1975 that he was selling oils 'wet' off the wall. Isherwood had a habit of stacking his 'wet' paintings one against the other and has sold more than one with the oils of one shaped with the pattern on the back of the board of another.

I suggested to him in 1976 that he may like to try painting with quick-drying acrylic paint, so I went to a shop, bought his range of colours in acrylic paint and returned with a canvas for him to try the paints on. He successfully dashed off a painting of 'The Guards at Buckingham Palace', one of his favourite themes, but he hated painting with acrylic paints. They dried far too quickly for Isherwood, who liked to shape the paint on the board or canvas using a number of techniques, including using his finger. I have this painting, one of the few Isherwood painted with acrylic paints, and it is one of the best I have seen of this subject.

From May through to November 1976 Lawrence and Pat spent a lot of time in Malta, in St Julian's Bay, where they held an exhibition that was opened by Pat on 14 July. Isherwood painted a portrait of the Prime Minister Dom Mintoff, which was presented to him on the occasion of his 60th birthday. Always with an eye for a pretty woman he painted Miss Malta too, in 1976.

In a long letter to Frank Carey, dated 7 September 1976, Pat reported several mishaps that had happened to them whilst away including a burglary at Lawrence's home in Wigan on 8 June. They did not hear about the burglary for about two months.

Lawrence reported to me in a letter dated 22 November that he liked Dom Mintoff's painting. In the same letter he reminded me that he would be 60 years old on 7 April 1977 and floated the idea of a retrospective exhibition of his work somewhere, perhaps at the University of Salford. The University were keen to go ahead but, sadly, we never got it organised – for various reasons. Lawrence was also negotiating to hold his 60th birthday show at the Scarisbrick Hotel and reported that he was trying to persuade Jean Alexander, who played Hilda Ogden in *Coronation Street*, to open it. It never happened.

I own a painting dated 1977, allegedly painted by Pat 'Isherwood' (it has her signature on it) of a boat at sea (it reminds me of a painting executed by L S Lowry), which I very much admire, but it is hard to believe that Isherwood didn't make a significant contribution to this painting. However, Pat was an accomplished painter in her own right. When Eileen and I visited Frank Carey in the Isle of Man in September 2011 we saw two of her still-life paintings of flowers; they had a distinctive style which was unlike that of Lawrence.

Lawrence and Pat returned from Malta to put on an exhibition in the Red Room at New College, Oxford. They put on another joint show of 90 paintings at the Scarisbrick Hotel in Southport, which opened on 9 December 1976 and included several paintings of scenes in Bolton. This was Isherwood's two hundredth exhibition. "They're destroying Wigan now", said Isherwood, "but Bolton still has a lot of the red-brick architecture and the mill scenes."

Isherwood mounted other exhibitions in the Museum of Fine Arts in Valetta, Malta, in Malaga and at the Galeria de Arte 27 in Torremolinos, Spain during their visits abroad.

PAT LOSES BRYNGWYDD FARM

Pat wrote in a Christmas card that they had arrived in North Wales on 16 December 1976. On 30 December Lawrence wrote to me and Merrilyn from Bryngwydd Farm, which they were in danger of losing to the executors of Kennedy White's will. Pat's husband had left most of his estate in trust for their two children. "Re Salford University I think I am too young to have a retrospective show – so as the negotiations are on (as you say in your card) we had better call it off I think. And we are HOPING to be in Italy then or Oxford? ...or in jail?" wrote Isherwood.

Bryngwydd Farm was sold with its 44 acres of freehold land by the executors whilst Pat and Lawrence were away in Malta. After returning home they barricaded themselves in the farmhouse as a protest because they believed that it had been sold at what Lawrence described in a letter to me dated 12 April 1977 at "a give-away price".

After I wrote to tell him that the University of Salford were going to arrange a retrospective show with the aid of an Arts Council Grant and that they would do it properly by collecting his best paintings from wherever they could be found, Lawrence changed his mind in a letter written to me on 29 April 1977, but it was too late.

Days later they returned to the Cervantes Hotel in Torremolinos. "Three weeks here have bored us" he wrote. Pat and Lawrence had purchased a 1970 Vauxhall Victor 'shooting brake', he announced, to transport his paintings to exhibitions.

In 1977 Pat took Lawrence on his first visit to Paris, where Montmartre and the Left Bank fascinated him as much in reality as they previously had in his imagination. Later, in the autumn of 1977, Isherwood held exhibitions in Oxford in the Oscar Wilde Room at Magdalen College (staying at the Eastgate Hotel) and at Pembroke College (staying at the Milton Arms).

Mary Robinson, a secretary at Salford Art Gallery, wrote to many of the artists who had held successful shows in Salford to ask whether they would donate one of their sculptures or paintings to the Friends of Salford Museums Association in order to raise money to improve the lighting in the rooms of the gallery, which was about to celebrate its 21st birthday. Characteristically, Lawrence donated one of his oils and they received donations from sixty other artists including Harold Riley (a protégée of L S Lowry), Olive Bagshaw, Pat Cooke and Pauline Vivienne. The show opened on Friday 28 July 1978 and ran until 3 September.

On the day of the opening Pat sent me a card from Torremolinos to say that they had occupied an apartment there since the beginning of June and that Lawrence had held a 'Jubilee Show' there at Galeria de Arte 27.

On 21 October 1978 Lawrence wrote to tell Frank Carey that he had been invited to judge the Miss Malta competition. Between 20 and 25 November 1978 Lawrence held an exhibition at the Oxford Students' Art Centre in Worcester Place whilst staying at the Tackley Hotel in High Street.

THE ISHERWOOD BALLROOM AND BANQUETING SUITE

In 1979, Frank and Marjorie Carey decided to dedicate the Cumberland Conference Room at the Scarisbrick Hotel to Isherwood, which became the Isherwood Ballroom and Banqueting Suite (the refurbished room had been open since October 1978). 200 of Isherwood's paintings were hung there for many years. Unfortunately, many of them were stolen by visitors to the hotel over several years and the exhibition eventually had to be taken down.

Stephen Taylor was asked to provide a life-size bust of Isherwood in 'cement fondue' and another one of his 'wife' Pat, which stood on pedestals at the entrance to the Isherwood Suite when it opened (they are now in the ownership of Frank Carey in the Isle of Man). A photograph of the sculptor, then aged 23, and the Isherwoods alongside the two busts appeared in the *Southport Visiter* on 21 January 1978. The room was officially opened on 1 March 1979. By this time the relationship between Pat and Lawrence had cooled considerably. At the opening Lawrence was, unusually, visibly inebriated.

ISHERWOOD AND PAT WHITE PART; MORE TIME IN BILLINGE HOSPITAL

Pat White and Lawrence separated in 1979. It turned out that they were not married after all. The 'marriage' had been another of Isherwood's publicity stunts. She was forced by the executors of her husband's will to move out of Roseacre on 22 August 1979 and occupied several properties on the Wirral after that until she died on 7 February 1996 at the age of 67. She lived in Oxton, Wirral at that time. Pat left two sons, Fraser and Cameron. Eileen and I met Fraser White at the launch of Stephen Eckersley's book *Isherwood.*

Shortly after the opening of the Isherwood Ballroom and Banqueting Suite at the Scarisbrick Hotel Frank Carey wrote to Lawrence on 18 April 1979 at Billinge Hospital:

> "Dear Plonky Isherwood,
>
> Good Lord! Bless my soul! Fancy you being in Hospital, but I hope you are now well on the road to recovery.

> I am enclosing all the Brochures [from the Isherwood Suite opening on 1 March 1979] that I have left, for your interest. I had no idea that you were in Hospital and why didn't you contact me when you went in four weeks ago instead of writing to the Manchester Evening News?
>
> It is only the quality of the food that is keeping the Isherwood Ballroom and Banqueting Suite going, as everybody complains about the wall coverings.
>
> I am delighted to note that you have signed your letter 'and Pat', and hope that you're getting everything sorted out. If I can do anything for you, please let me know."

Lawrence appreciated Frank's style of humour as well as his straightforward manner.

On 23 April 1979 Pat dumped 'all his stuff' in Wigan. She promised, according to a letter that Lawrence wrote on 23 April 1979, to have his car delivered to Wigan as well.

I received a brief note from Lawrence, dated 11 May 1979, to say that he was expecting to be out of hospital in a week. He had been binge drinking again. An additional problem was that he faced several large bills that needed paying.

I visited him at the hospital during his second stay there. "I was drinking up to two bottles of whisky and some wine every day" he told the press. "Even during the night I was up every half an hour to have a drink." He was told by the hospital that another drink would kill him.

He believed he and Pat would get back together, but

admitted in a letter he wrote to me from hospital, dated 15 May, that his drinking had probably driven her mad. When Isherwood met Pat White he told her that he was not an alcoholic as her husband had been, and she encouraged him to start drinking again, moderately at first. He hoped that Pat, who was trying to sell Roseacre, would come and live with him in Wigan. "I do MISS her – I really have a broken heart!" he wrote to us.

Merrilyn and I collected him from Billinge Hospital and took him out for a meal at the Withins, a pub-restaurant in Bolton, on 28 May 1979. Lawrence wrote to me from D1 Ward (the alcoholic unit) at Billinge Hospital in a letter postmarked 20 August 1979 to tell me that Pat had taken him there for further treatment shortly after the Isherwood Ballroom and Banqueting Suite was opened at the Scarisbrick Hotel. On 21 September 1979 he announced to Frank Carey "I'm stone cold sober now". He was still a patient at Billinge Hospital in October 1979 but left in time to organise another show in November.

THE ISHERWOOD GALLERY: FINANCIAL PROBLEMS LOOM

Starting in September 1979, Lawrence wrote to us on headed notepaper from 151 Wigan Lane, which had been rebranded as 'The Isherwood Gallery'.

A three-day one-man show featuring over 100 of his paintings was held by Isherwood at the Brocket Arms Hotel in Mesnes Road, Wigan, and ran from 25-27th November 1979. It wasn't one of his successful shows, according to a letter that 'Ishy' wrote to us on 28 December 1979.

An article appeared in the *Wigan Post and Chronicle*, dated 12 January 1980, to announce that Lawrence had opened the 'Isherwood Gallery' in his home. On 19 January he wrote a letter to Frank Carey to complain about his financial position. Wigan Council had issued a 'distraint order' on him for £289 unpaid rates, he owed over £1,000 to a bank and had his utility bills to clear. It was a plea for help. Pat, he alleged, still held some of his 'stuff' including his woolly vests.

Isherwood called off an exhibition at the Scarisbrick Hotel which he had planned for 15-17th February 1980. He suffered bad health after the Brocket show and his letters of this period are full of self-pity.

On 7 March he wrote to tell me that he had sent four paintings to the TSB Bank in Wigan to join 12 'bundles' of paintings that were already stored there, but the manager, Mr Aldridge, had sent them back and asked him to remove all his paintings from the bank's vaults. Pat and Lawrence had a joint account with the TSB which had become overdrawn, but Lawrence cleared the debt by selling two life insurance policies. He also paid an overdrawn account with Lloyds Bank in Chester.

Isherwood was still in financial difficulties at this time, so he advertised in the *Daily Telegraph* – 'Ish needs cash to exist' - and offered 20 oil paintings at £20 each. As a result the paper produced an article on Isherwood that resulted in people knocking on the door of 'Leywood' ('The Isherwood Gallery') for weeks. After that he put a 'No Callers' notice on his front door and asked people to call only by appointment.

On 2 March 1980, an article appeared in the *Sunday People* about Isherwood being down on his luck again. "I recently needed a new pair of glasses, for instance. The bill was £75, which I didn't have so, I paid the optician in oils. I've used paintings to buy groceries, to pay printing bills, builder's bills – all sorts of things" he told reporter Val MacDermid.

Isherwood raised nearly £500 by mounting a show in his local newsagents shop and exchanged an oil painting entitled 'London's Rotten Row' for £20 worth of groceries at a shop in Mesnes Road, Wigan.

Harry and Lily Isherwood had left all they owned to their two sons, Lawrence and Gordon. Mother Lily and Lawrence's income was supplemented by rents from properties, several shops and a house, that the family owned. When Lily died Lawrence collected these rents for a while without splitting the income with his brother Gordon, who didn't seem to mind this arrangement. However, when Lawrence went to live with Pat White on the Wirral the rents didn't get collected until Molly Isherwood decided to take matters into her own hands and started collecting them again. After one of the houses had been renovated with the help of a Government grant, it was sold and the proceeds were paid into the Britannia Building Society and split equally between the two Isherwood brothers, as Harry and Lily had intended.

On 19 March 1980, Isherwood wrote to say that he was receiving letters from Pat White and that he still missed her. He was trying to open accounts with the Yorkshire and Co-operative Banks and was learning Spanish from cassettes. "Don't call please unless you ring – I'm quite OK – philosophising etc – I've too much to do – without my painting – which I've **got** to do. I show in Windsor about June", he wrote.

His mood improved when he heard that Nadia would be back in Britain between May and September 1980. They met and Lawrence claimed that Nadia would be writing his biography. She left for Australia on 9 September 1980.

Lawrence often said that he would write his autobiography and dedicate it to his mother, but he never did.

On 3 August 1980 he sent me a card to tell me that he had had the clutch on his car repaired and driven himself to Aberystwyth, where he was staying in the Gwalia Hotel on the North Parade. He claimed to be there writing his autobiography and announced that his brother Gordon was a granddad for the first time. His nephew Clive's wife Marguerite had given birth to a boy. Lawrence sold paintings to guests staying at the hotel, including one to a 'Professor from Philadelphia'. In Aberystwyth he was treated for pernicious anaemia.

In a letter dated 16 April 1980 his headed notepaper was changed; 'The Isherwood Gallery' became 'The Isherwood Collection'. Apparently, Wigan Council was attempting to charge him business rates.

In October 1980 he was back at the Scarisbrick Hotel "varnishing and cleaning" the Isherwoods in the Carey collection. In October 1980 he wrote to Frank Carey from the Gwalia Hotel in Aberystwyth. He mentioned a 21-year-old women called Juliet, who he met on his visits to Aberystwyth, in several letters at this time.

Our next correspondence from Lawrence, apart from a Christmas card, was in May 1981, when he told us that he had been to see a play at the Octagon Theatre which he clearly didn't enjoy. His car was giving him trouble again and Nadia Weiner had promised to hold a retrospective exhibition of his paintings in Sydney on 31 May 1981. Merrilyn and I invited him to stay with us in Bolton in July 1981 and we all went to the Octagon Theatre together. I drove him back to Wigan with homemade cakes and marmalade.

In a note written on Nadia's birthday (4 October 1981) in red biro he told me that he was to have another show in the Knowsley Room at the Scarisbrick Hotel in Southport. The exhibition 'Homage to Picasso', Isherwood's two hundred and fourth show, ran for two days (20-21st October). It was held to commemorate Picasso's 100th birthday. Despite help with the publicity from 'Southport Corporation' he only took £170. It was his first show for two years.

A postcard from Lawrence dated 2 August 1982 informed us that he was appearing on the Granada TV programme *Yesterday* on 5 August talking about Goya. "My first break into my NEW life – after 65 etc. Younger than springtime" he wrote, again in red biro.

Another 'red biro letter' arrived, dated 7 August 1982, on which he had spilled coffee, which was almost unreadable. He wrote: "It's been a FUNNY pattern this year. April 3 – came out of hospital [I wasn't aware until this letter arrived that he had been readmitted for a third time in March 1982]. April 16 to Juliet – Tour, Weymouth, Longleat, London etc – 1,000 miles – then I broke down in Welsh hills – worked with Aberystwyth University..."

It sounded as though Isherwood was very active in the first half of 1982. He signed his letter off with 'OAP'.

ISHERWOOD HITS ROCK BOTTOM

Another letter, typed (unusually, and badly), arrived, dated 5 November 1982, which indicated that Isherwood's mood had swung into despair again. He had received a court order for £430 of unpaid rates. He had been to the Scarisbrick Hotel, but Frank Carey was away and he hadn't had a very happy visit ("I got lots of wine"). He was having trouble with his car again: "...tax disc ran out on 31 October... and they've taken my TV away due to 'her [Pat's] car's arrears'" he wrote.

Another 'red biro letter' arrived, dated 5 December 1982, in which he told me that he had attended a charity auction for the International Spinal Research Trust in Prestwich at which two of his donated paintings fetched £245 (18" x 24") and £145 (12" x 16") in an auction, which pleased him. He also told me: "Am applying for public assistance as I can't exist on £18 weekly with ALL MY BILLS. I owe £1,000."

In a letter he wrote to us in blue biro on 22 February 1983 Lawrence explained that the DHSS in Wigan had refused his application for benefits on the grounds that he had been advertising the sale of paintings worth £2,000. He was expecting to go to a DHSS tribunal in Bolton backed by a statement from his psychiatrist, Dr Maragakis, at Billinge Hospital. "I can't eat my pictures". His car was parked at the side of his house, broken down, which prevented him travelling. The tone of his letter suggested that Lawrence was in a bad way both physically and mentally.

In a letter addressed to Frank Carey, dated 23 May 1983, he also mentioned the DHSS assessment and wrote: "You are a lovely man Frank and you've done me good. I don't think I could go on without a VISIT to you. I like to watch HOW you manage people also – your personality."

There is no doubt that Frank Carey played an important role in the life of James Lawrence Isherwood. The Carey family, Frank, Marjory, Mark and Jill, helped Lawrence through some of the most difficult times in his life. On the occasion of Frank's 43rd birthday on 19 August 1975, when Lawrence was 58, Frank received a tape that Lawrence had recorded as a birthday present which expressed his emotions about the Carey family, especially Frank, which Frank retained.

Lawrence's next typed letter to us, dated 14 June 1983, announced that he had been to a DHSS tribunal in Manchester and had been granted 'benefits'. He had been at the Scarisbrick Hotel in Southport for a week and been to a first night at the Octagon Theatre. Lawrence wasn't painting much at this time.

FIRE DESTROYS ISHERWOOD'S PAINTINGS AT 'LEYWOOD'

In July 1983, when Isherwood was 66, tragedy struck (see *Manchester Evening News* dated 5 July 1983); a fire in the kitchen caused considerable damage at 'Leywood'. A fire-brigade spokesman said: "A spark from a gas cooker ignited hardwood panelling. That caused the fire to spread quickly."

The blaze destroyed hundreds of Isherwood's paintings including 'The Lancashire Madonna', a large oil painting that had been exhibited at several Isherwood exhibitions including the one that I organised at the University of Salford in 1975. Isherwood told Don Frame at the *Manchester Evening News*: "I seem to be fated. Some years ago I was involved in a bad car crash. I have been burgled three times. All sorts of other things have gone wrong."

Molly and Gordon Isherwood were out to dinner at a restaurant on the top of Parbold Hill when they heard about the fire at 151 Wigan Lane and left to see what they could do to help Lawrence.

Lawrence had just completed a commission to paint a portrait of Lord Weymouth at Longleat, which temporarily alleviated his financial problems: "I was beginning to feel quite pleased with myself again and now this. I feel like shooting myself. Maybe it's just the spur I need to get going again. I had been tailing off a bit but this is giving me the creative urge to begin painting again."

Come what may, 'Ishy' never forgot to send me, Merrilyn and the children a Christmas card. In 1983 we received a handmade one from him.

He was distraught after the fire at his home and, after that, became more or less a recluse; he shut himself off from the rest of the world and we saw very little of him. He was drinking heavily again at this time. His letters to us came less frequently after the fire. We received none in 1984.

Lawrence was suitably suited and booted to attend a black tie 'Non-Stop International Gala Evening', held on Sunday 12 February 1984 at the Library Theatre in Manchester to raise money for the Greater Manchester Committee of the International Spinal Research Trust. He persuaded Frank and Marjorie Carey to make available a holiday for two at the Scarisbrick Hotel as a raffle prize.

In his letters written to Frank Carey in the 1980s Lawrence mentioned his fixation on the actress Georgina Hale.

Sadly, Frank and Marjorie Carey separated, and Frank moved out of Southport to live in Blackpool in 1986. After a few years he decided to set up home in the Old School House in Laxey, Isle of Man. He purchased Brown's Cafe and Tea Room in Laxey, near the Laxey Wheel, and demolished and rebuilt the premises. With hard work it was turned into one of the most thriving businesses on the Isle of Man.

I kept in touch with Frank after he left Southport, and Eileen and I visited him at his home in Ramsey in September 2011. Today he is an accomplished composer of music who awaits discovery by the music industry. His greatest triumph to date is the recording of 'Pacific Moonlight', a strict tempo and sequence dance selection of 12 tracks by the 42-piece Francis John Dance Orchestra (see the website www.careymusic.co.uk).

Marjorie Carey, with whom we have also kept in touch, lived at the Scarisbrick Hotel until the summer of 2011, when the hotel ran into financial difficulties again. She still lives in Southport. Tragically, their son Mark died, and Eileen and I attended his funeral in Southport on 7 August 2006, the last time I saw the Carey family together.

In a letter dated 10 December 1985 Lawrence admitted that the fire had been traumatic for him, not to mention his "BOOZE problem". He wrote:

> "I am fighting NORWEB at present – am writing to the M/C [Manchester] Evening News – to say the 'Economy 7' isn't cheap. I've got a bill for £1,000. I've got to pay £25 a week. £1,840 for 1986. I think they've put the Infirmary [across the road from 'Leywood'] on my account. It's taking all my fire insurance money – the Bolton office treated me like 'dirt'..... The meter that was on was booking everything down at high rate – instead of white meter – **this** I had to fight."

We picked Lawrence up to spend some time with him over the Whitsuntide holiday weekend in 1986 and he wrote to thank us on 23 May 1986. That was the only letter he wrote to us in 1986, although he did send us an article that appeared in the *Lancashire Evening Post* of 6 November 1986, which announced that he was planning an exhibition at Wigan Pier in 1987 to mark both his 70th birthday and the 100th anniversary of the family shoe business. His brother Gordon owned two shops in Wigan, one in Wallgate and the other in Darlington Street.

Frank Carey received several holiday postcards from Lawrence in 1986, sent from the Costa Del Sol, mainly from Torremolinos, and signed 'Gladys'.

ISHERWOOD'S SEVENTIETH BIRTHDAY

Isherwood was 70 years old on 7 April 1987, but there was no party for him, presumably because he was away again on his travels. At year end he sent us a calendar published by World Travel Centres which, as well as celebrating his birthday and the 100th anniversary of the family shoe business, displayed a reproduction of 'The Lancashire Mine'.

We received a postcard from him dated 17 June 1987; he was staying at the Miami Hotel in Torremolinos and planning another show at the Brocket Arms in Wigan. In a letter that we received from Lawrence dated 27 July 1987 he wrote:

> "I am ready to go back to Spain. I had a good DO this time and sold 12 paintings – am becoming a 'GIGOLO' but was robbed on the last day at the hotel. With 2 hrs to airport? I'd been out to a beach party near Gibraltar – which I didn't want to go to. 'Experience' that's all – put it down to...."

Clearly 'Ishy' was beginning to get some pleasure out of life again.

151 Wigan Lane is separated from the adjacent Bellingham Hotel by an unmade private road that leads also to a tennis club at the rear of the property. Lawrence had regular complaints from the management of the hotel because he parked his car on this private road, which also gave access to a car park at the

rear of the hotel. The hotel saw this as an obstruction. When the hotel applied for planning permission in 1988 to extend the business Isherwood went to war with them.

"Bellingham Drive is a private passage and unsuitable for the amount of traffic and vehicles coming and going to the hotel" he told the *Manchester Evening News* (9 June 1988). "I am the main objector [to the planning application] as my house catches it in every way. Massive lorries and coaches also use this passage going to the Bellingham. Rats cross over from waste bags that they put out at the back. My car has been hit several times by the incessant traffic."

Despite a deferment, Wigan's Planning Committee approved this planning application.

Our last communication from James Lawrence Isherwood was a handmade Christmas card in 1988.

I SAY GOODBYE TO LAWRENCE

Gordon Isherwood (his brother) telephoned me on the 7 June 1989 to say that Lawrence had asked me to visit him in Billinge Hospital and I did so, on the evening of the 8 June. Lawrence didn't look to me as though he would die the following day. We had a cheerful discussion, with a few laughs, and he made a remarkable request of me. "Help me to stand up to take a pee", he said and, with a bit of effort, I granted him one of his last wishes.

Frank Carey visited Lawrence in the afternoon of the 8 June. Molly Isherwood, his sister-in-law, told me later that we were the only people Lawrence had asked to see outside his immediate family before he died.

Gordon and Molly Isherwood, who visited him every day

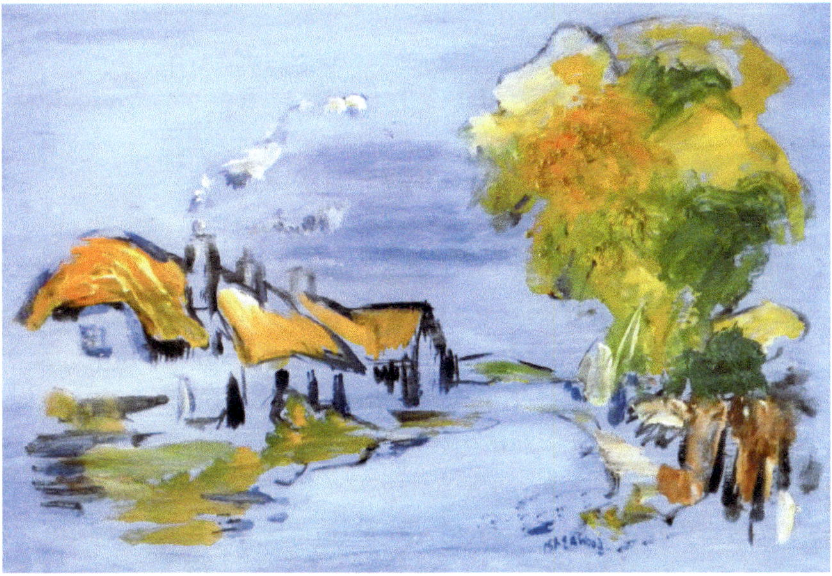

Devon Cottage (oil on board; 35 x 45 cm).

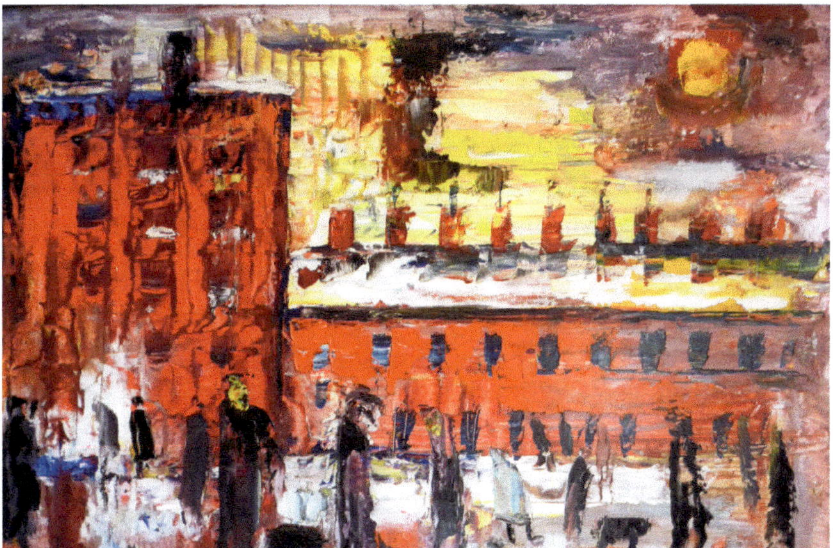

Wigan Stocking Factory (1962, oil on board, 45 x 60 cm).

during the weeks when Lawrence was cared for in Billinge Hospital, and their son Clive, were with him when he passed away at 9.20 pm on Friday 9 June 1989 from bowel cancer, aged 72.

FUNERAL AND OBITUARIES

Several local and national newspapers carried obituaries including *The Independent* (19 June), the *Wigan Observer* (15 June) (Isherwood's nephew Clive invited Geoffrey Shryhane to write both of these obituaries), The London *Evening Standard* (20 June), *The Guardian* (29 June), *The Daily Telegraph* (14 June), and the *Manchester Evening News* (16 June; appropriately written by Andrew Grimes). In a report of his death in the *Bolton Evening News* of 12 June 1989 I said of my friend: "I think he was one of the greatest unrecognised artists in Britain."

Eileen (my second wife) and I were two of the few people (less than 20) who attended his funeral at Wigan All Saints' Parish Church and his burial in Gidlow Cemetery (off the A49) on 16 June 1989, a beautiful summer Friday. Pat White was there and Merrilyn, my first wife, sent flowers. Frank Carey had booked a holiday in Spain, so he was away at the time of the funeral. Lawrence is buried with his father, Harry Lawrence Isherwood, who died on 25 April 1955 at the age of 67, and his beloved mother Lily, who died on 24 July 1971 at the age of 79.

Merrilyn and I never lost contact with 'Ishy'; we tried to keep him going and to raise his spirits. When he was hard up I offered to buy paintings from him, but it wasn't easy. He would try to give me a painting that I was willing to pay a good price for. I gave him cheques for paintings that we had

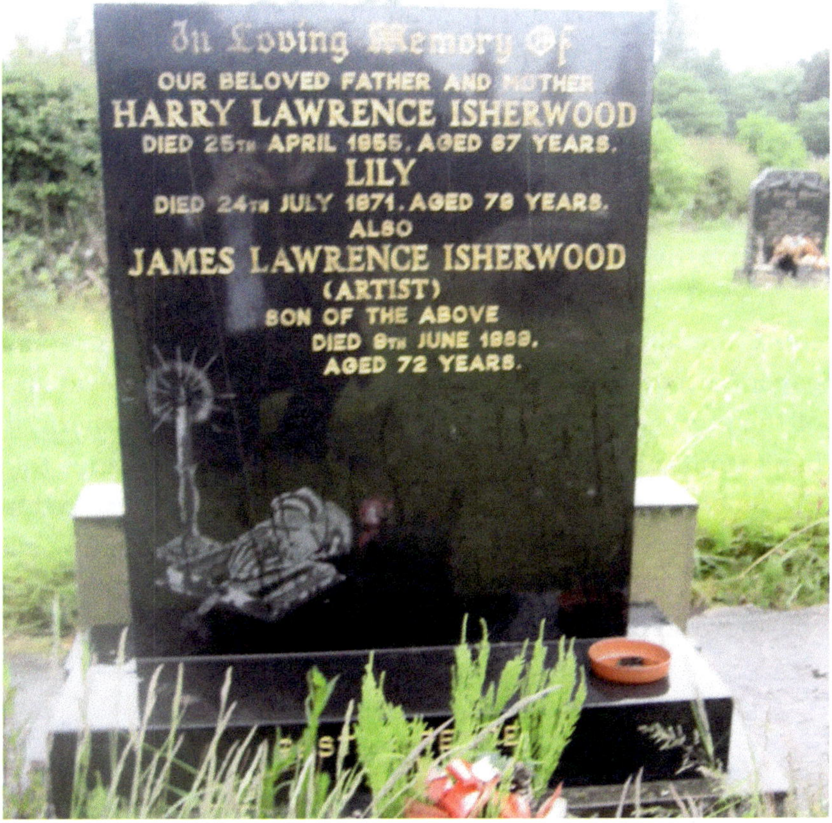

The Isherwood family grave in Gidlow Cemetery, Wigan.

agreed a price on and he would tear the cheques up. I just left the paintings in his house with a feeling of regret. We could have both benefited from these transactions. He badly needed the money.

Even after the fire in July 1983, the downstairs front room of his house had many small paintings stored in it. I came across a lovely watercolour of Lord Street, Southport which I would have paid anything for because it was a scene painted close to Christ Church, where I went to secondary school from 1951 to 1956. I tried to buy an oil painting entitled 'Devon Cottage' but he wouldn't accept any money for it. After Lawrence died and I told the family I was willing to purchase this painting from them, they found it at 'Leywood' and very kindly presented it to me for all the support that Merrilyn and I and our girls, Sally and Sheena and, later Eileen, had given Lawrence over many years. I treasure it greatly.

After Lawrence's death it took Molly Isherwood and her son Clive almost a decade to go through the paintings and papers recovered from 'Leywood'. They came across evidence of the storage of Isherwood paintings, over 300 of them, in bank vaults and decided to sell some of them. Lawrence told me shortly after I met him that his best works were stored in bank vaults for posterity. I do hope the Isherwood family has kept the best of his bank vault collection, all stored there with the approval of Mother Lily.

WIGAN RECOGNISES ISHERWOOD AS THE HISTORY SHOP OPENS

On 23 July 1992, Eileen and I were present when the Mayor of Wigan officially opened the 'History Shop' (today it is the 'Museum of Wigan Life') in a former library at the junction of Library Street and Rodney Street, Wigan, where their first temporary exhibition 'Isherwood – Local Artist, Local Life', the first exhibition of his work since his death, was held along with a preview of 'Wigan Heritage Service's Exhibition' to celebrate the opening. George Orwell studied in this building - Wigan's former library - in 1936. By this time Gordon Isherwood was suffering from Parkinson's disease, but he was able to attend the exhibition in a wheelchair.

This exhibition of Isherwood's paintings was open to the public from 24 July to 5 September 1992. The poster for the exhibition displayed a portrait of Mother Lily, painted in 1965, and the organisers produced a pack containing a short biography of Isherwood illustrated with reproductions of some of his paintings. Lawrence had requested that none of his paintings be sold until three years elapsed following his death; none of the paintings on display at this exhibition were for sale.

About this exhibition fine art consultant W (Bill) H Lacey wrote:

> "Lawrence Isherwood was not an artist to follow the latest trends or pander to the whims of prospective buyers. His work is unique and shows an integrity seldom found today. I have no doubt that this exhibition will be controversial, Isherwood paintings always have been. It is not possible to look at these paintings and not to react....this exhibition allows a new generation to make up its own mind."

EXHIBITIONS OF ISHERWOOD'S WORK AFTER HIS DEATH

I attended an exhibition at Stockport Art Gallery which the Wigan journalist Geoffrey Shryhane opened on 22 October 1993. It ran from 23 October until 17 November. Bill Lacey was there too.

The *Wigan Observer* announced the death of Gordon Isherwood on 14 December 1993. Like his brother Lawrence, Gordon died of cancer. Aged 73, he was cremated on 15 December 1993. Molly Isherwood closed the Isherwood shoe business down, the end of a long tradition of the family manufacturing and selling shoes in Wigan.

After that Molly kept Eileen and me informed of all the exhibitions that she and her son Clive and his wife Marguerite helped to organise in letters dated 14 January 1994, 23 March 1994, 12 September 1998 and 5 December 1998 as well as by postcard and telephone, for which I have been grateful.

I was unable to attend the private view of the 'Northern Art Show' on Monday 28 February 1994 at the Mall Galleries, near Trafalgar Square in London, which George Melly the jazz singer opened. The show, which was open to the public from 1-6th March, featured 42 of Isherwood's paintings. Lawrence's painting of *Coronation Street* stars, executed in 1961, was shown at this exhibition but it was not for sale. Significantly Molly's sister Florence, who was married for a short period to Isherwood, attended this London show.

George Melly said:

> "On occasions, Isherwood bows to his old friend L S Lowry and, looking at the pictures on show tonight, we see a painter totally curious about life and the way to translate that life into images on a flat surface. Sometimes he fails. But, when he succeeds, he does so tremendously. An artist who doesn't fail cannot triumph. At his best Isherwood is amazing."

The London show was followed immediately by another in Liverpool at the Opimian Gallery, with a private view held on Friday 25 March 1994, where 11 of Isherwood's paintings were on exhibition.

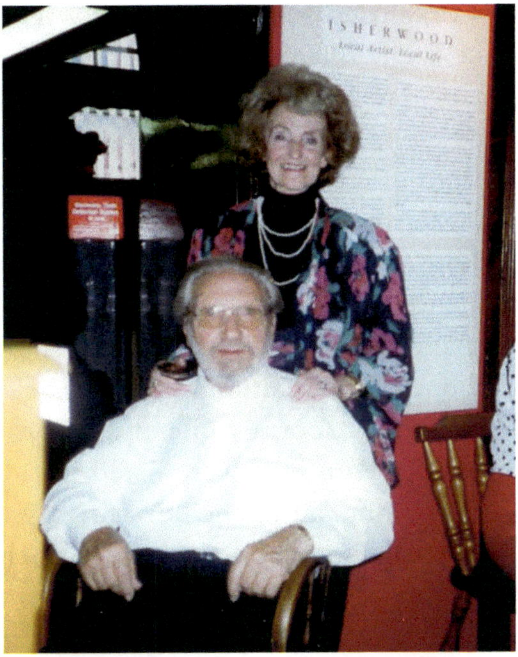

Molly and Gordon Isherwood at the opening of Wigan's History Shop in 1992.

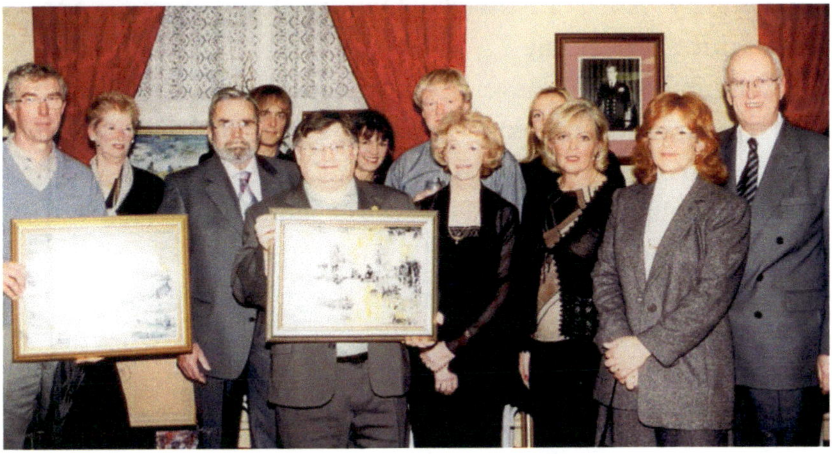

Ian McCartney MP (Molly Isherwood on his left, her son, Clive, standing behind) at the opening of the show at Wigan Town Hall in 2002. Eileen and Dr. Brian Iddon are on the right of the picture and Fraser and Mandy White are standing behind Ian McCartney.

The Isherwood family organised several shows at Wigan Town Hall after Lawrence died. Eileen and I attended the private view of a show on Friday 17 November 1994, which Molly Isherwood organised along with her son Clive and his wife Marguerite in the Atrium of Wigan Town Hall in Library Street. It was a one-day show for the general public on Saturday 18 November. When the show opened to the public 300 works of art were sold in the first three hours. More works were put on display in the afternoon and all those were sold as well.

Eileen and I missed the one-day exhibition which was held on Saturday 5 August 1995 in the Osborne Suite of the Royal Clifton Hotel in Southport. 85 Paintings were listed in the catalogue including 16 watercolours and pencil drawings. We also missed the private viewing of another one-day show (open to the public on 18 November) in the Atrium of Wigan Town Hall on Friday 17 November 1995. This exhibition was opened by Auril Fishwick, Deputy Lord Lieutenant of Lancashire at the time.

When Tony and Beverly Callaghan opened their new bar and restaurant 'Number 15' on King Street West in Wigan they decided to open the 'Isherwood Suite' on the top floor so they could display all their Isherwood collection (see *Wigan Observer* of 30 November and 8 December 1998).

Molly invited Eileen and me to the private viewing of 'Into the Millennium', which was held at Wigan Town Hall on Friday 12 November 1999, but I can't remember attending (see the coverage by David Ward in *The Guardian* of 15 November 1999). We attended the private view of another show ('The Last Show') at Wigan Town Hall, which was opened officially by Ian McCartney (Member of Parliament for Ashton-in-Makerfield) on 15 November 2002. We paid £450 for a framed oil painting of 'Mevagissey Harbour'.

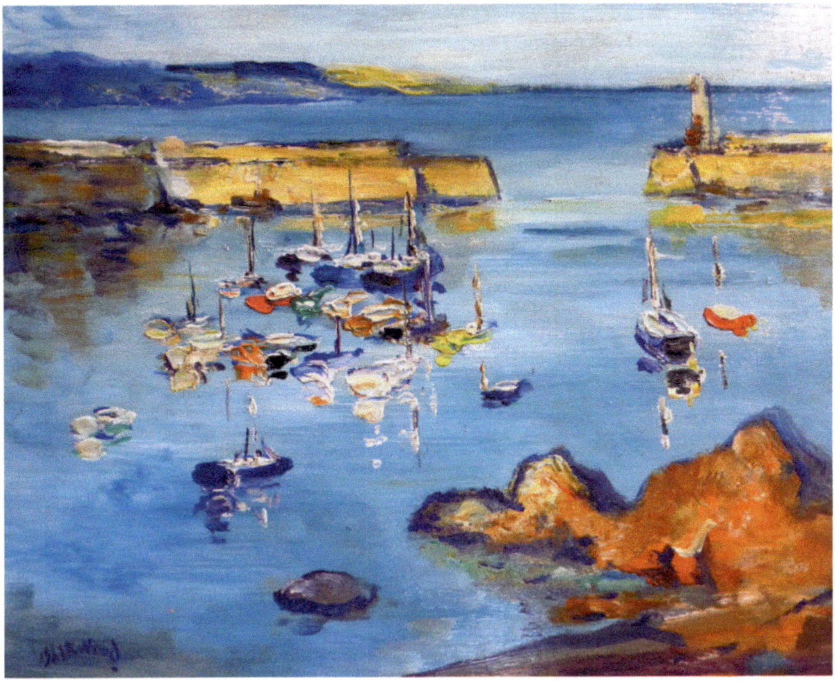

Mevagissey (1963; oil on board; 28 x 32 cm).

I missed the private viewing of a second exhibition of Isherwood's paintings ('Unseen Paintings from the Archives') held at the Mill House Gallery in the Old Windmill, Mill Lane, Parbold on Friday 18 November 2005 but attended another there on 10 October 2008, which I have referred to in the opening paragraphs of this book. An oil on board painting of 'Guards at Buckingham Palace', which featured on the invitation card, was sold to an Irish art dealer for £6,000.

The 20th episode of the 29th series of BBC1s *Antiques Road Show*, which was recorded in Southport and broadcast on 25 February 2007, valued an Isherwood landscape at £700, a seascape at £1,500 and a picture of the *Coronation Street* character Ena Sharples in the Rover's Return at £1,500.

Exhibitions were held at Colin de Rouffignac Antiques in Standish with private viewings on Friday 21 November 2008 and Friday 27 April 2012, which we also missed. We couldn't attend a show on 3 July 2009 because Eileen's son Lee and his partner Lillian were visiting us from Gran Canaria.

The last exhibition of Isherwood paintings that I attended was at Wigan Town Hall on Saturday 19 June 2010. It was a weekend sale of 'Northern Art', but most of the paintings on display were Isherwoods.

The Turnpike Gallery in Leigh exhibited 50 of Isherwood's oil paintings from the William ('Billy') Higham Collection between 2 November 2010 and 2 January 2011. Both Billy and Bunty Higham (his wife), who were florists in Wigan, were keen collectors of Isherwood's paintings.

INTEREST IN ISHERWOOD'S PAINTINGS CONTINUES

Isherwood, who always sold his paintings at 'affordable prices', would be surprised by the prices his paintings are fetching on the open market today. As I write (May 2011) the highest price for the sale of an Isherwood that I have come across is £8,000.

His paintings are regularly on sale on the internet, both by private individuals on ebay and by private dealers, either on ebay or on their own websites. By 'googling' James Lawrence Isherwood on 11 May 2011 I came across 45 entries on the internet; there are more today. There is an official website which leads to a short biography written by Geoffrey Shryhane, a video on Isherwood talking about his paintings, works of art for sale, an art gallery showing many of Isherwood's paintings listed under themes, photographs of the artist and contact details at www.isherwoodgallery.co.uk (this site also gives links to other websites). On the website www.isherwoodart.co.uk can be found a rare U-Tube video (in four parts) in which Frank Booth interviews Isherwood about several of his paintings. 14 Isherwood paintings can be found on the website www.bbc.co.uk/arts/yourpaintings.

Lawrence always threatened to write his autobiography, which he said would be entitled 'Mother Lily – A Tribute to Her' and would pull no punches about his chaotic life style. It never appeared, so I have written this book as a tribute not only to his mother but to others who supported him and especially to the artist himself.

Molly Isherwood told me that they have lots of exercise books in their archives in which Lawrence recorded incidents in his life along with comments, some vitriolic, about the various people he knew. When these archives are made available publicly, a complete biography about Isherwood the artist will no doubt be written. I am pleased to say that he never spoke badly either of myself or Frank Carey, according to Molly Isherwood.

His work is in many permanent collections, which include those of Wigan, Salford, Stoke, Stockport, Hereford, Coventry, Warrington and Northampton and many of the colleges at Oxford and Cambridge Universities, as well as the collections of hundreds of private individuals.

Some fake Isherwoods have been identified on the market, so beware. Indeed, I have seen several paintings attributed to Isherwood on sale on the internet which looked to me like fake Isherwoods. Those of us who have been close to Isherwood during his lifetime would probably be able to spot a fake. Examples of suspected fake Isherwood paintings can be found on the websites I have mentioned above.

It's time now for a retrospective exhibition in a leading art gallery to show the best of the work of James Lawrence Isherwood. I hope I can live long enough to see it.

NOTES

1. A paperback reprint of the Eckersley book *Isherwood* was launched at The Room Four conference venue in Golborne on Friday 22 March 2013.

2. Wigan and Leigh College began in 1858 as Wigan Mining and Technical School. In 1974 it changed its name to Wigan College of Technology, then, in 1993, it merged with Leigh College and adopted its present name.

3. Margaret Purchase tells the story in her dissertation on Isherwood of Martin Ryan, a Wigan rugby league footballer who often visited the Leylands' shoe shop, inviting Isherwood to hold an exhibition in his public house the Balcarres Arms which is in Haigh. There is an Earl of Balcarres public house at the junction of Scholes and Greenhough Street and I believe it is more likely that Isherwood held an early one-man show there.

4. The Wigan journalist Geoffrey Shryhane was a friend of Lily and James Lawrence Isherwood for twenty years before he fell out with 'Jim'. In his book *Wigan and Wiganers*, Book Clearance Centre, 2006, he included a short chapter (pp. 68-74) on Isherwood.

5. L S Lowry left most of his wealth to Carol Spiers, a former art teacher, who called him 'Uncle'. Her mother Martha Lowry introduced Carol to Lowry when she was 13, and he became a regular visitor to their flat in Rochdale. Hence, this visitor to the University of Salford exhibition was probably Martha Lowry.

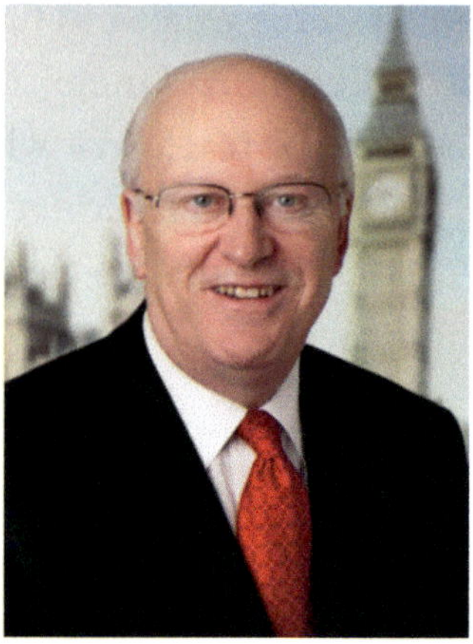

ABOUT THE AUTHOR

Brian Iddon was born on the West Lancashire Plain in Tarleton and educated at Tarleton C of E Primary School, Christ Church Boys' Secondary Modern School and the Technical College in Southport, and at the University of Hull from where he graduated in 1961 with a BSc in Honours Chemistry. He was awarded a PhD by the university in 1964 and a DSc in 1981.

He was employed teaching and researching chemistry at the Universities of Durham (1964-1966) and Salford (1966-1997) and became well-known for presenting a demonstration lecture 'The Magic of Chemistry' throughout Britain and in Europe.

Brian was elected to Bolton MB Council in 1977 and held various positions and served several committees of the Council until 1997 when he was elected to Parliament in the safe Labour seat of Bolton, South East, from which he retired in

2010. He was Chairman of Bolton's Housing Committee from 1986 to 1996.

Brian's interests in Parliament covered a multitude of topics in the education, health and social services, housing, home affairs and science and technology policy areas. He grasped some controversial subjects such as the policy on illicit drugs, euthanasia, legislation surrounding health food products, the Middle East Peace Process and Kashmir. He helped to steer through three Acts of Parliament and was a Member of the Science and Technology Select Committee.

Today, apart from his various writing projects, he holds a number of voluntary posts in the science policy area, in education and with a community charity.

BV - #0078 - 170626 - C116 - 229/152/5 - PB - 9781861511515 - Matt Lamination